EASY to DRAW
Anime & Manga
FACES + EMOTIONS

This Book Belongs to:

....

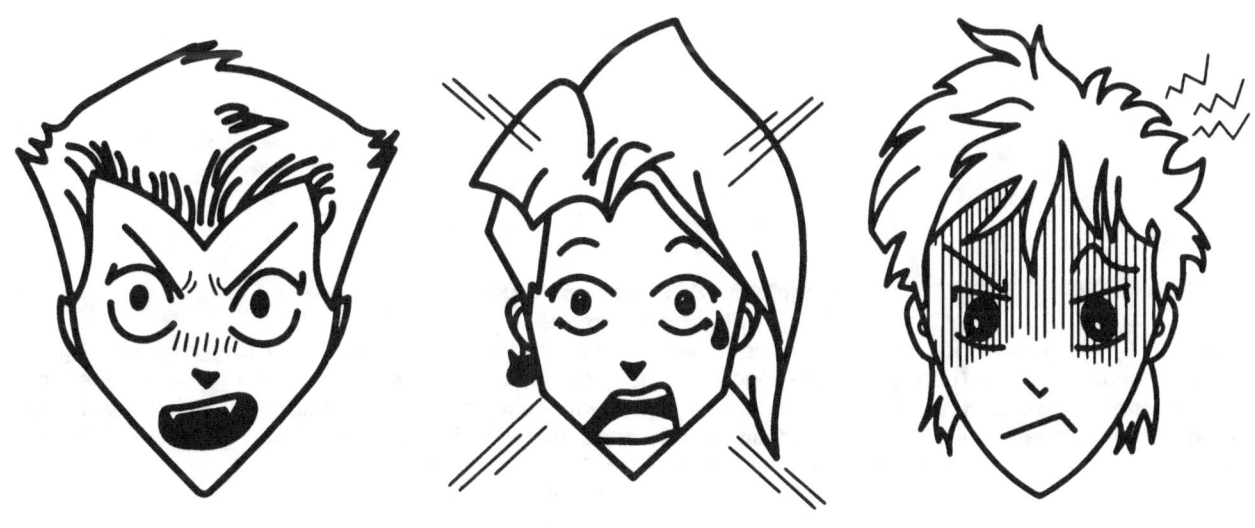

Sunlife Drawing

Are you a fan of ANIME & MANGA? Are you looking for a DRAWING TUTORIAL of Anime FACES and EMOTIONS?

This book is a great choice for you! It is a STEP by STEP guide that will show you how EASY to DRAW 28 different Anime & Manga EMOTIONS on various FACES. You will be ABLE to DRAW each face in just 5 EASY to follow STEPS. In addition, there are short INSTRUCTION of the main distinctive futures for every face. It will help you to UNDERSTAND the DIFFERENCE between various emotions and will make the DRAWING process EASIER and INTERESTING.

Grab this book and ENJOY DRAWING!

Copyright © 2017 by Sunlife Drawing
All rights reserved.
No part of this publication may be reproduced, distributed, or transmitted in any form or by any means, including photocopying, recording, or other electronic or mechanical methods, without the prior written permission of the author, except in the case of brief quotations embodied in critical reviews and certain other noncommercial uses permitted by copyright law.
Paperback Books: amazon.com/author/sunlifedrawing
Printable Books: etsy.com/shop/sunlifedrawing
Facebook: fb.me/sunlifedrawingbooks
Twitter: twitter.com/sunlifedrawing
E-mail: sunlifedrawing@gmail.com

CONTENTS:

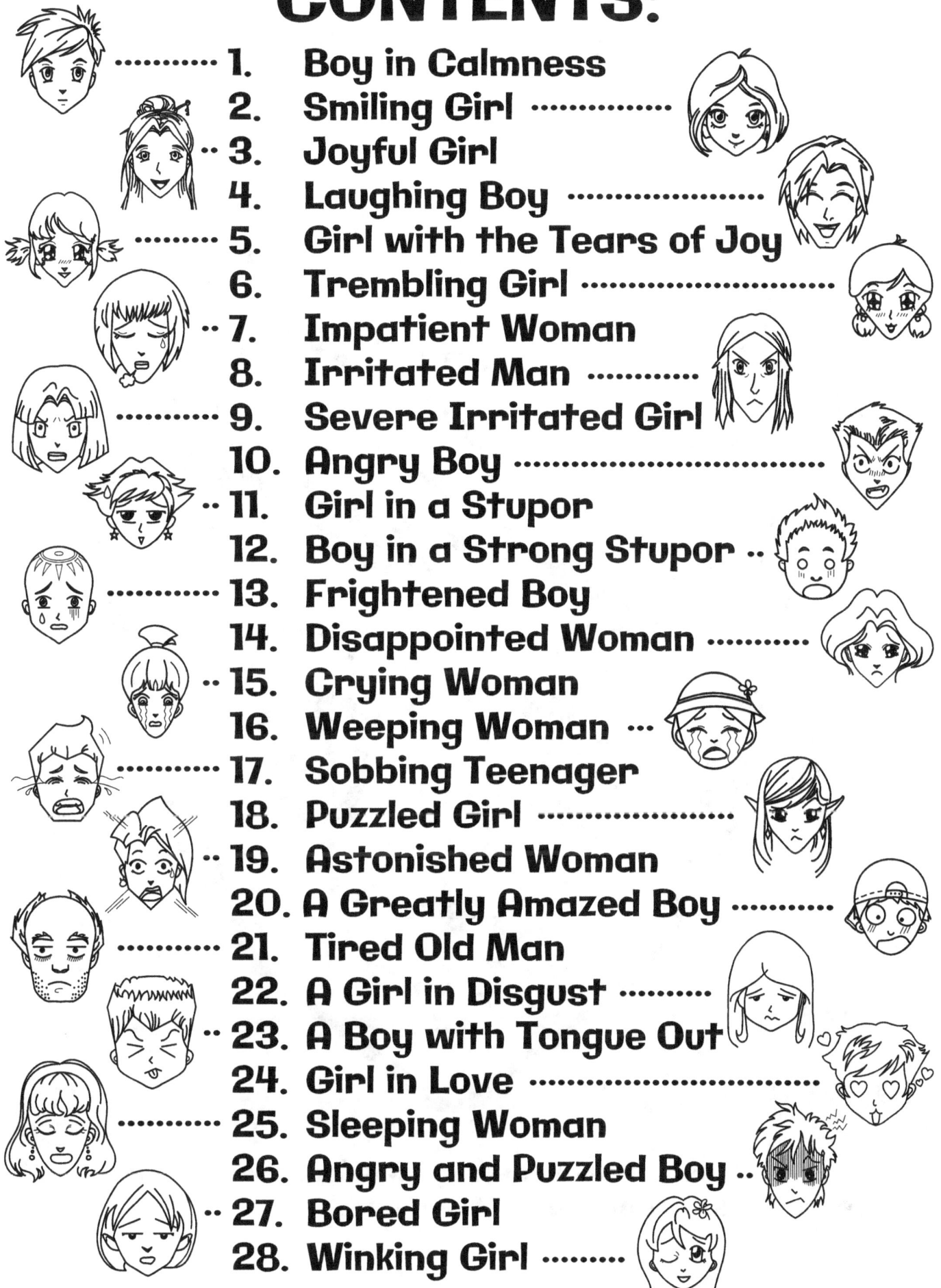

1. Boy in Calmness
2. Smiling Girl
3. Joyful Girl
4. Laughing Boy
5. Girl with the Tears of Joy
6. Trembling Girl
7. Impatient Woman
8. Irritated Man
9. Severe Irritated Girl
10. Angry Boy
11. Girl in a Stupor
12. Boy in a Strong Stupor
13. Frightened Boy
14. Disappointed Woman
15. Crying Woman
16. Weeping Woman
17. Sobbing Teenager
18. Puzzled Girl
19. Astonished Woman
20. A Greatly Amazed Boy
21. Tired Old Man
22. A Girl in Disgust
23. A Boy with Tongue Out
24. Girl in Love
25. Sleeping Woman
26. Angry and Puzzled Boy
27. Bored Girl
28. Winking Girl

1. Boy in Calmness

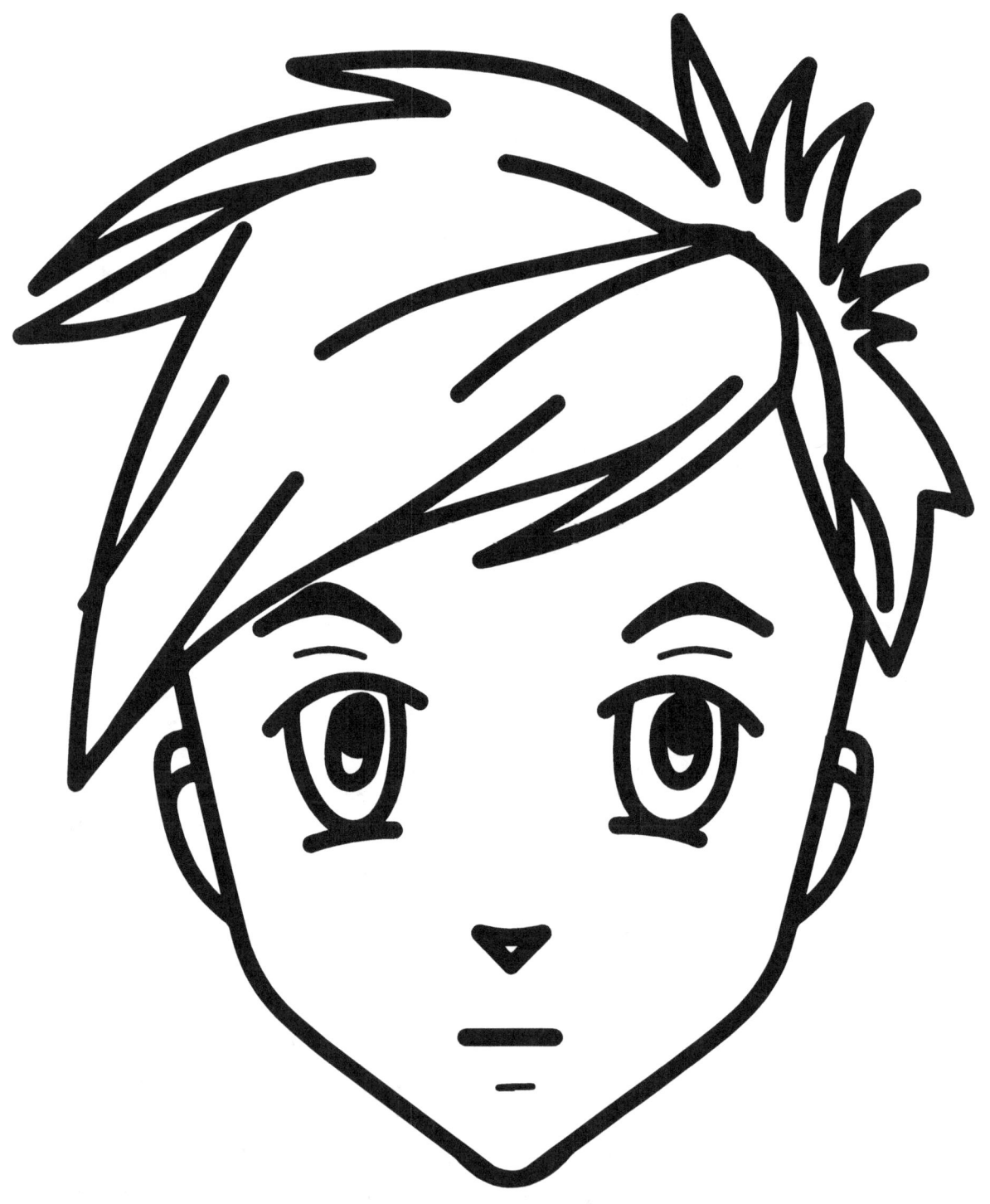

Face does not express any emotion. The distinctive feature: straight line for the mouth.

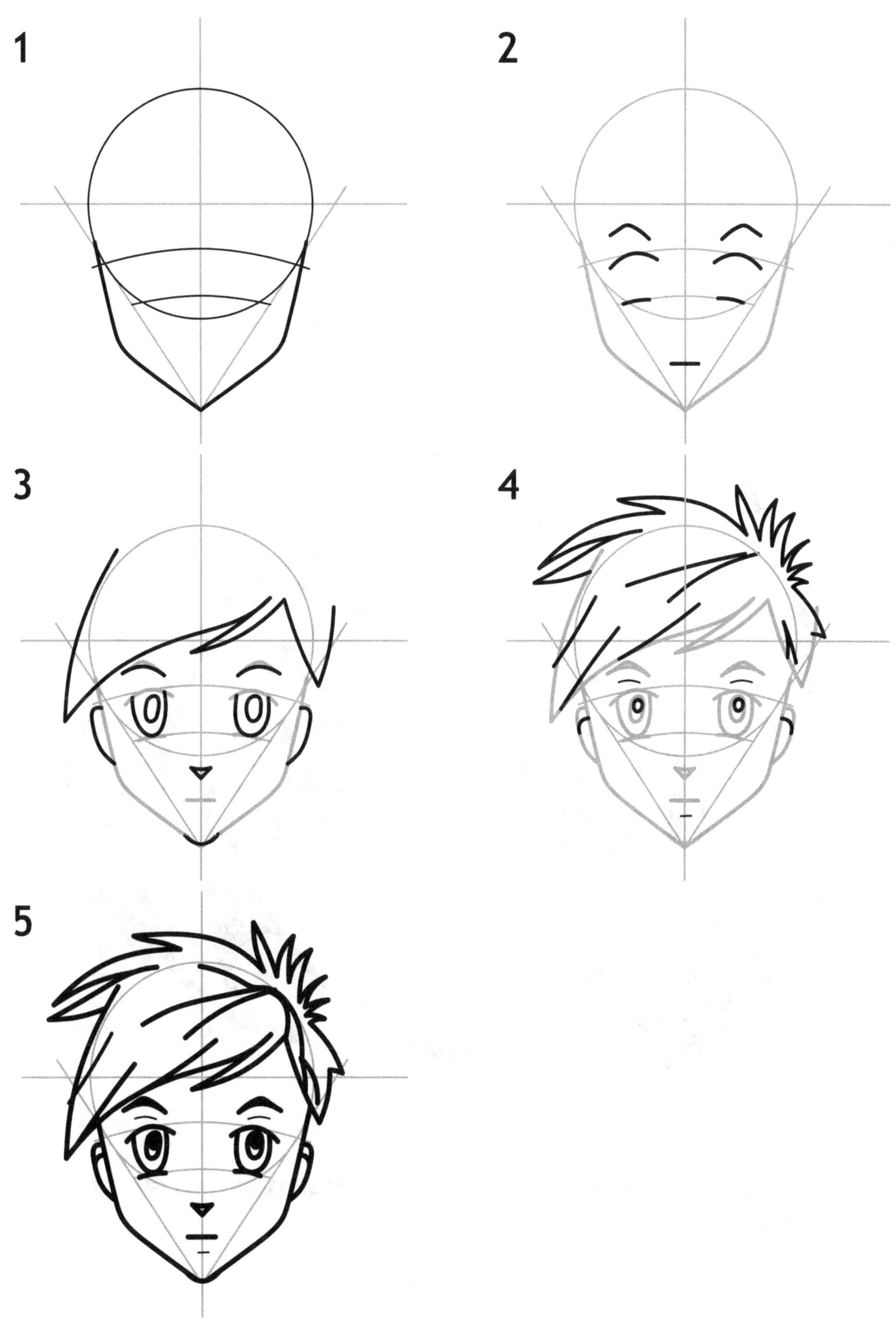

2. Smiling Girl

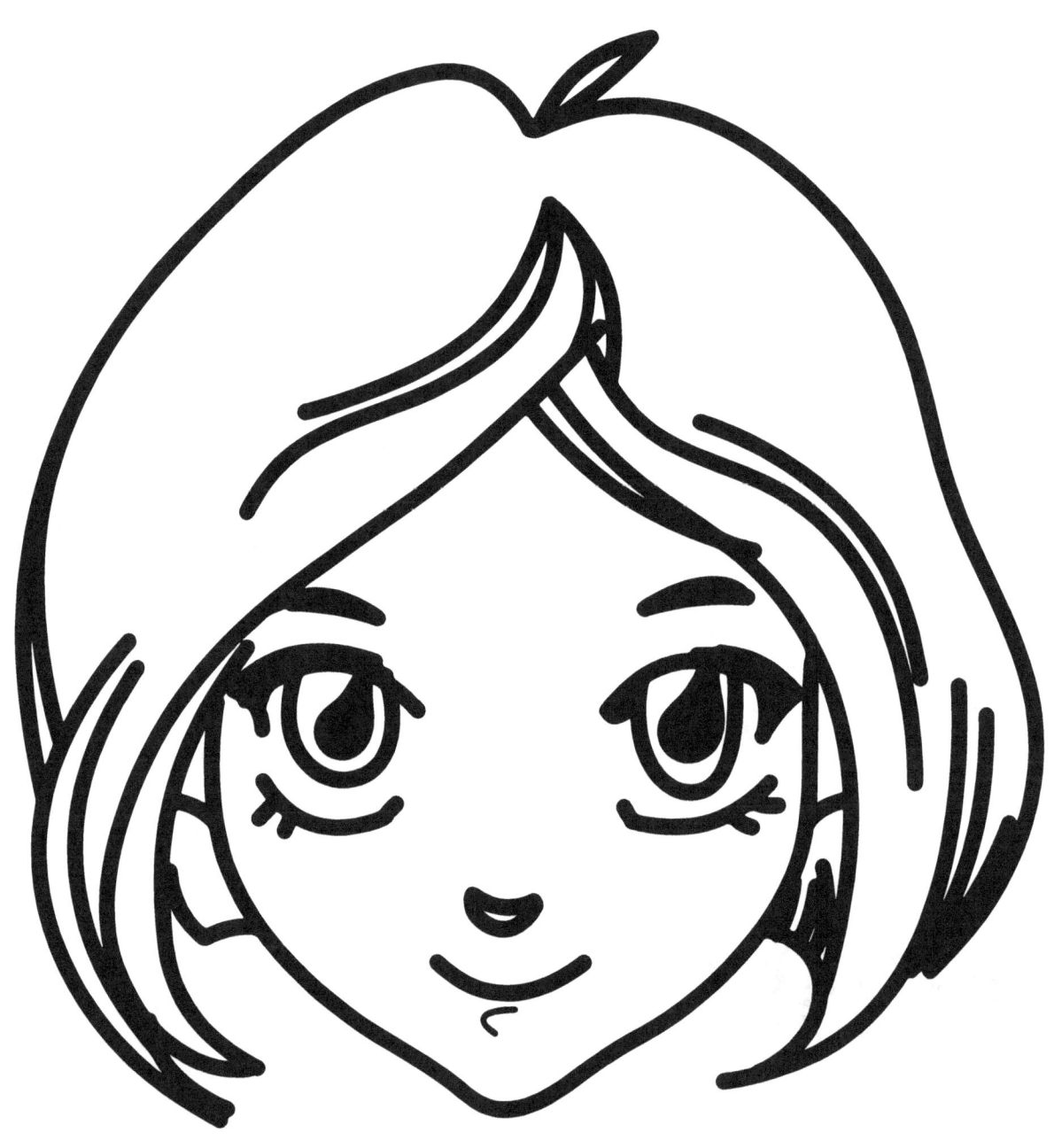

The distinctive feature: mouth drawn with a slightly curved line.

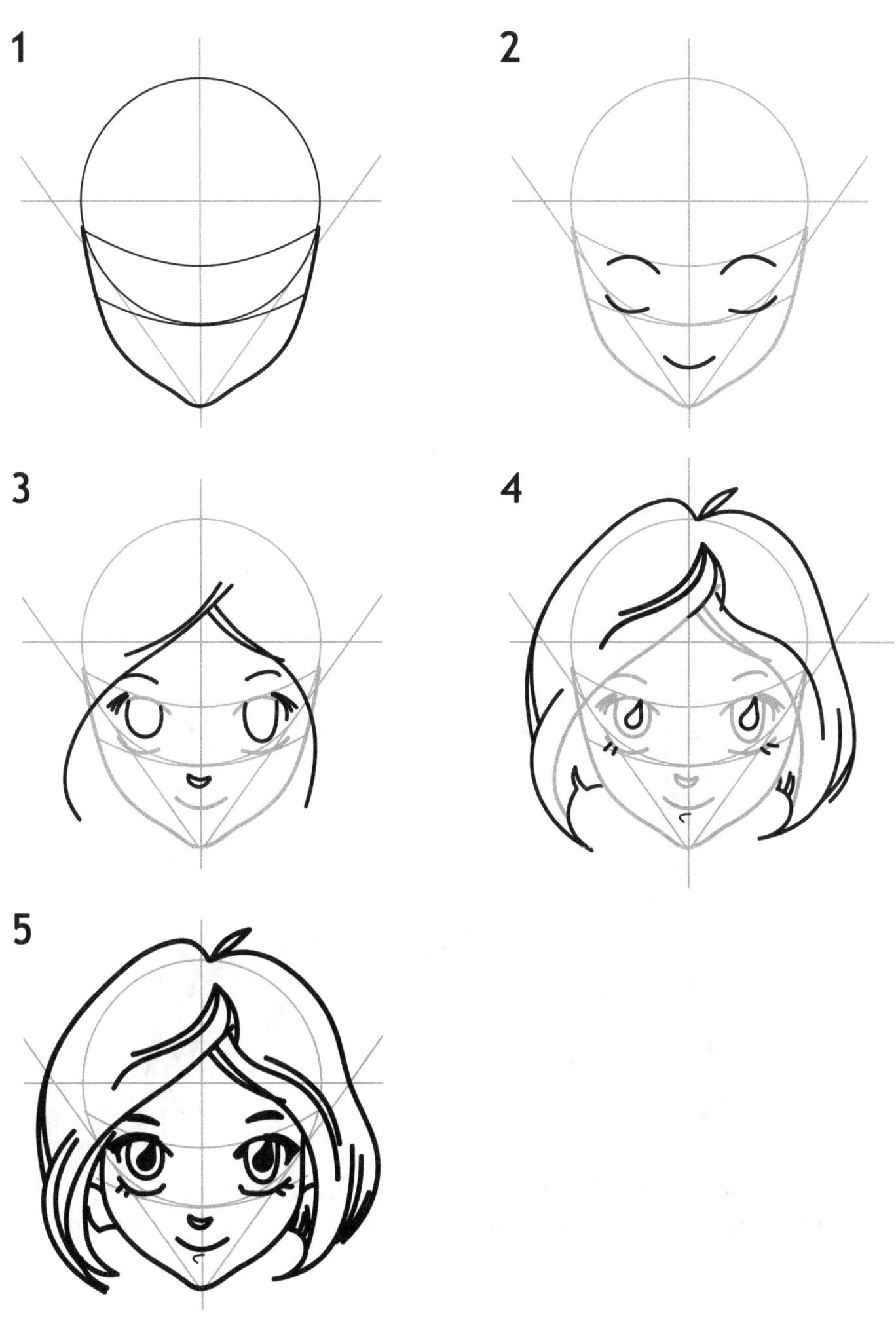

3. Joyful Girl

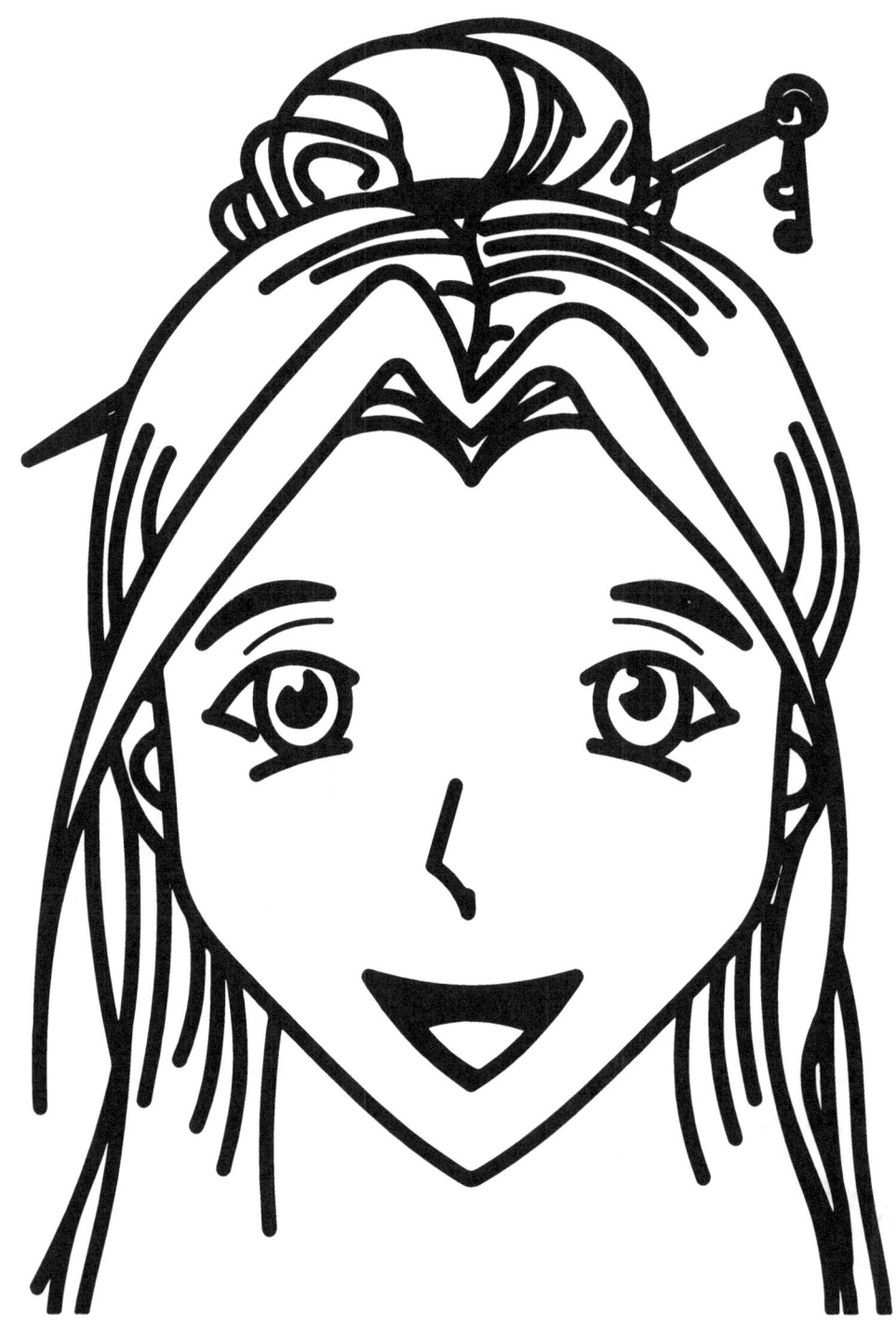

The lower eyelid of the eye covers the bottom of the iris. The mouth is similar to the shape of the inverted letter "D".

1

2

3

4

5

4. Laughing Boy

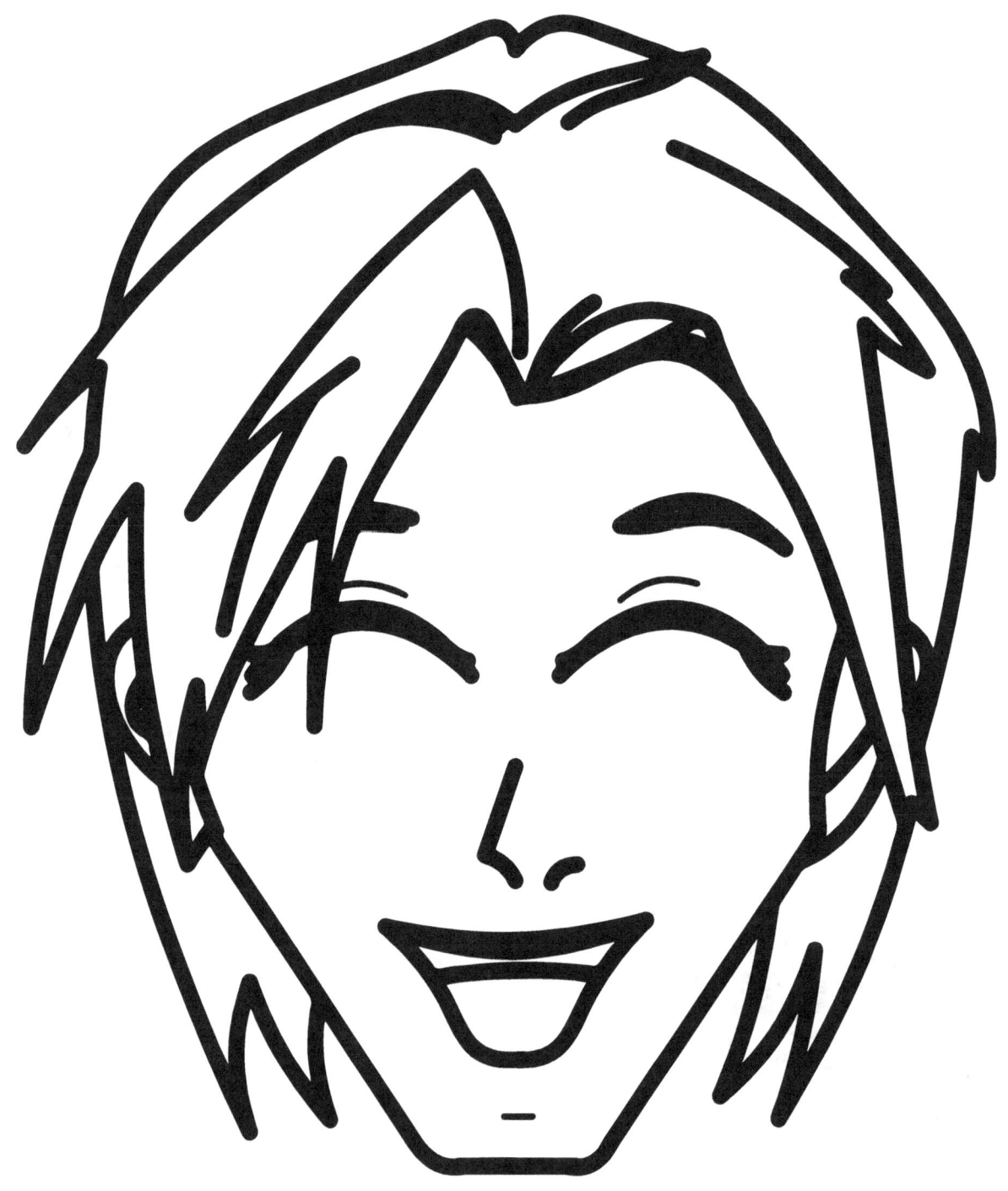

Eyes are screwed up with an arc-shape upwards. The mouth is similar to the shape of the inverted "D", but now it is larger.

1

2

3

4

5

5. Girl with the Tears of Joy

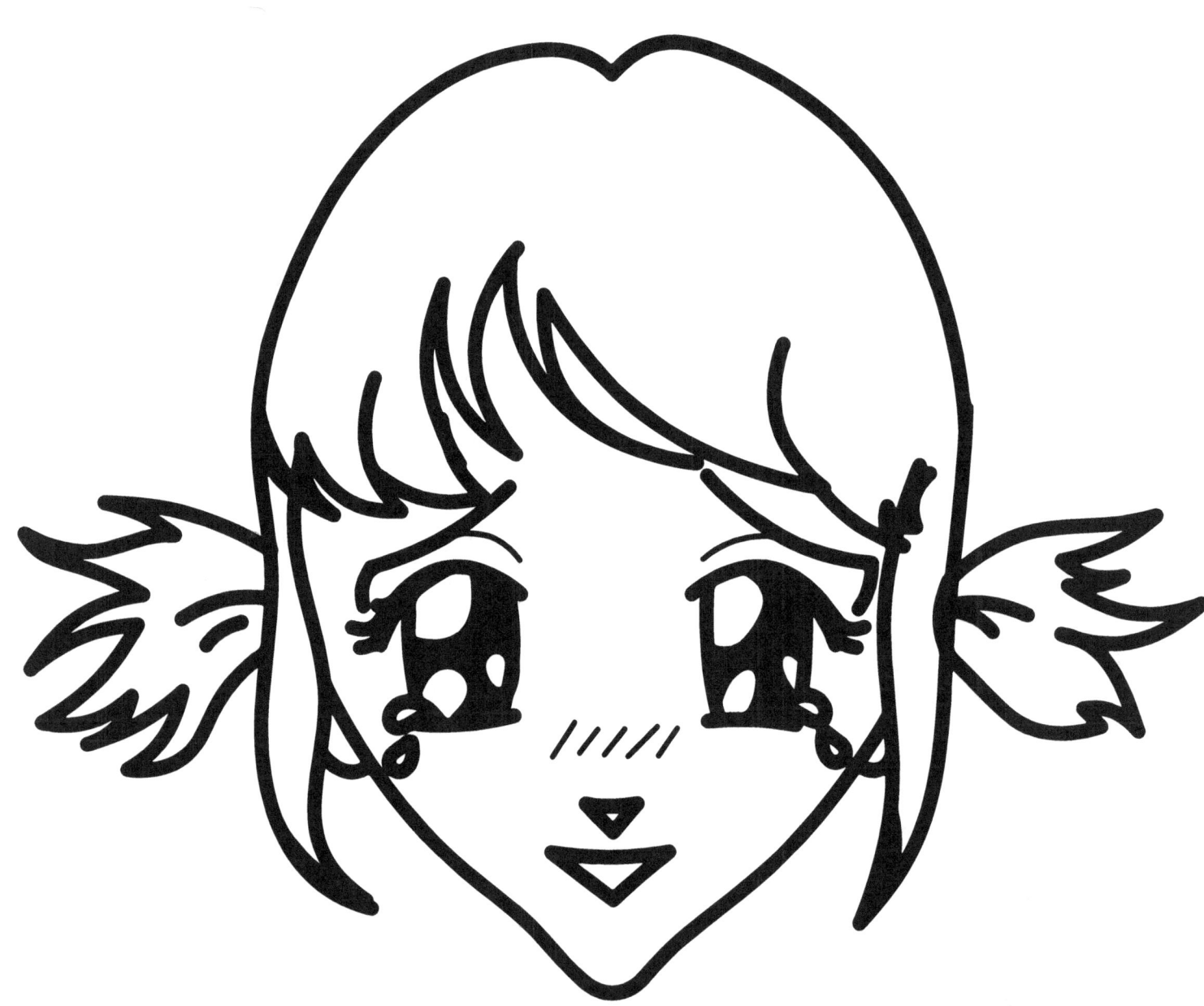

Eyebrows are cast down. Eyes are drawn with the large pupils in the corners with small droplets of tears. The mouth is similar to the shape of the inverted letter "D".

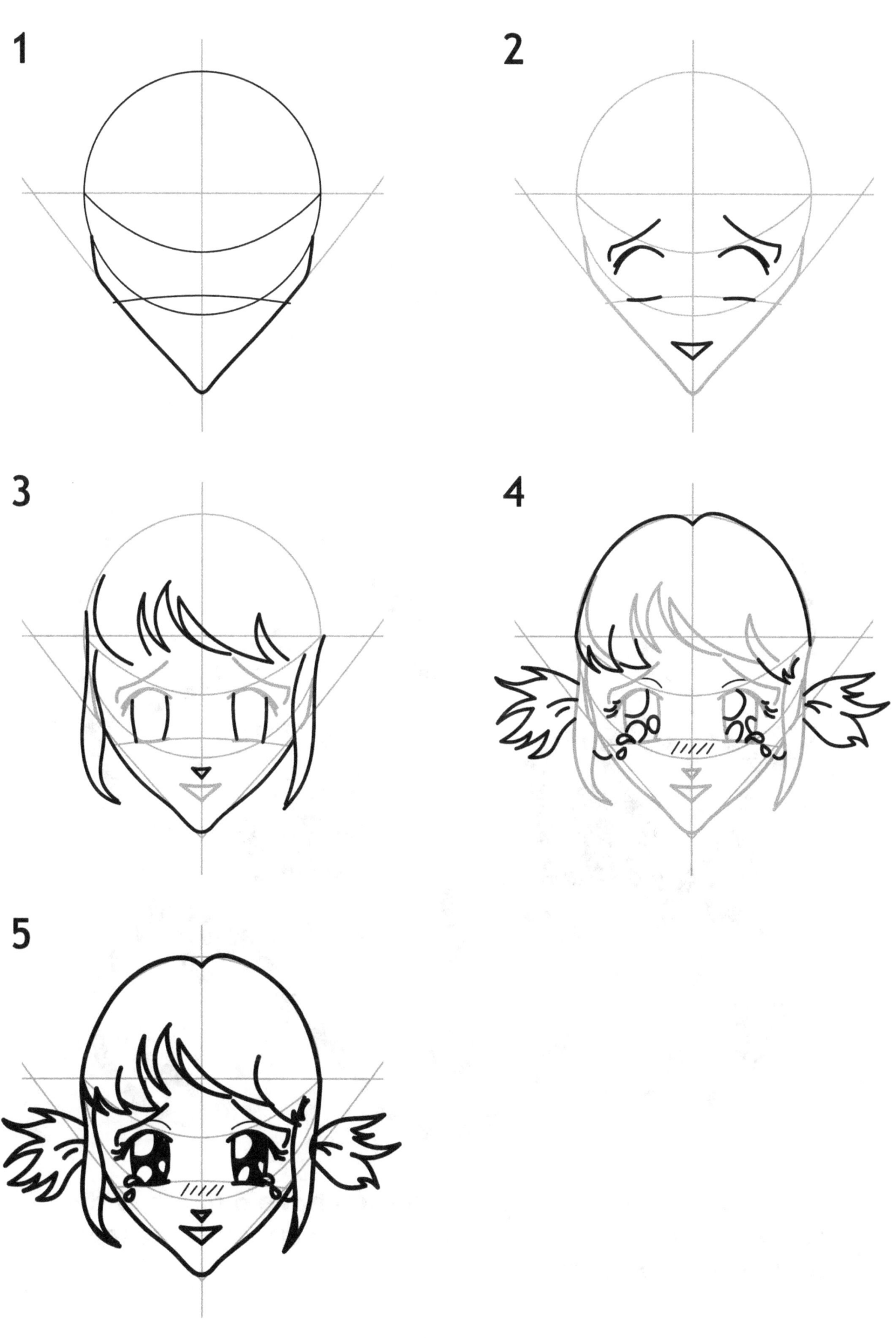

6. Trembling Girl

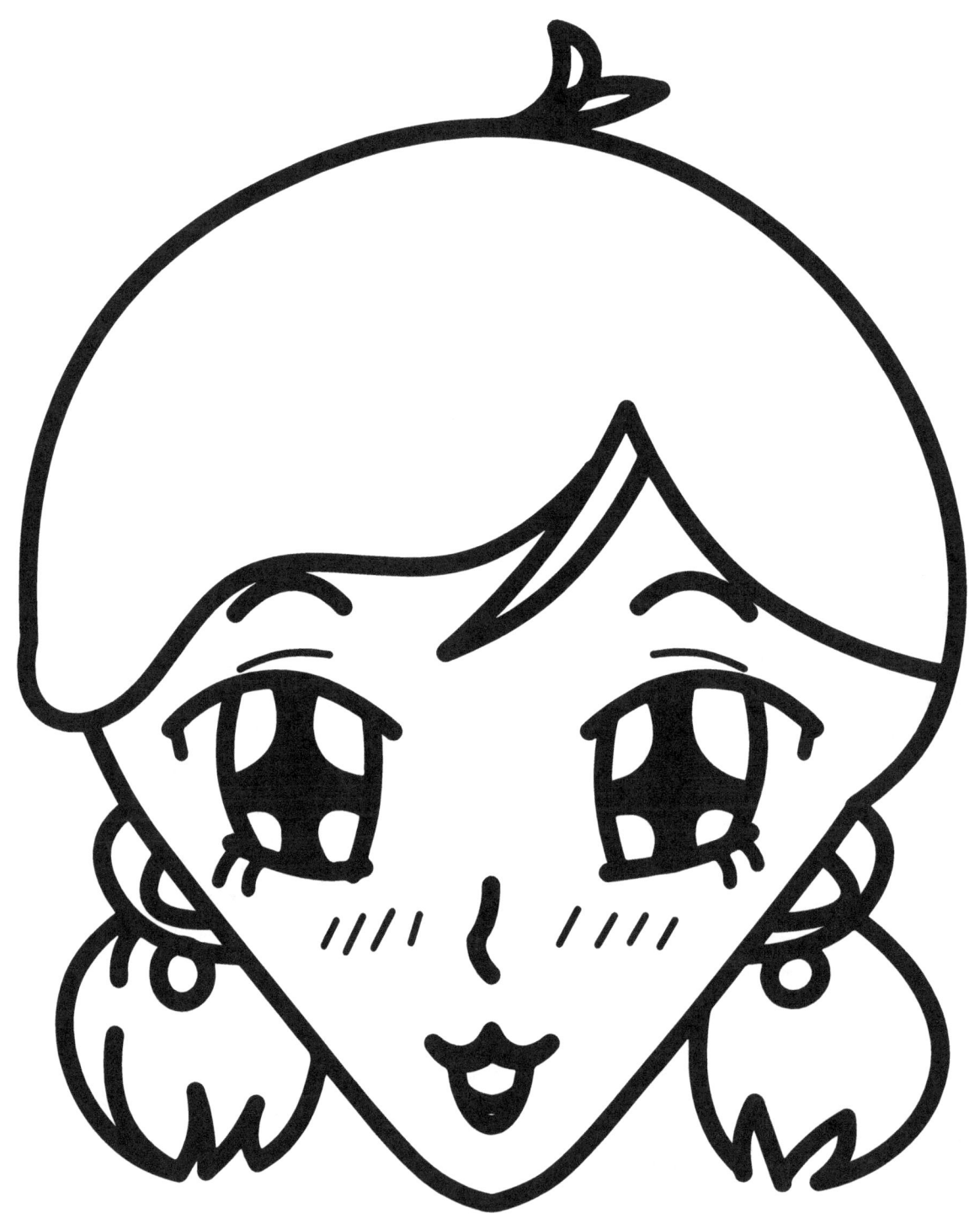

The pupils are enlarged and they have a glare in the form of a star-shaped rhombus. The upper lip resembles the shape of "W".

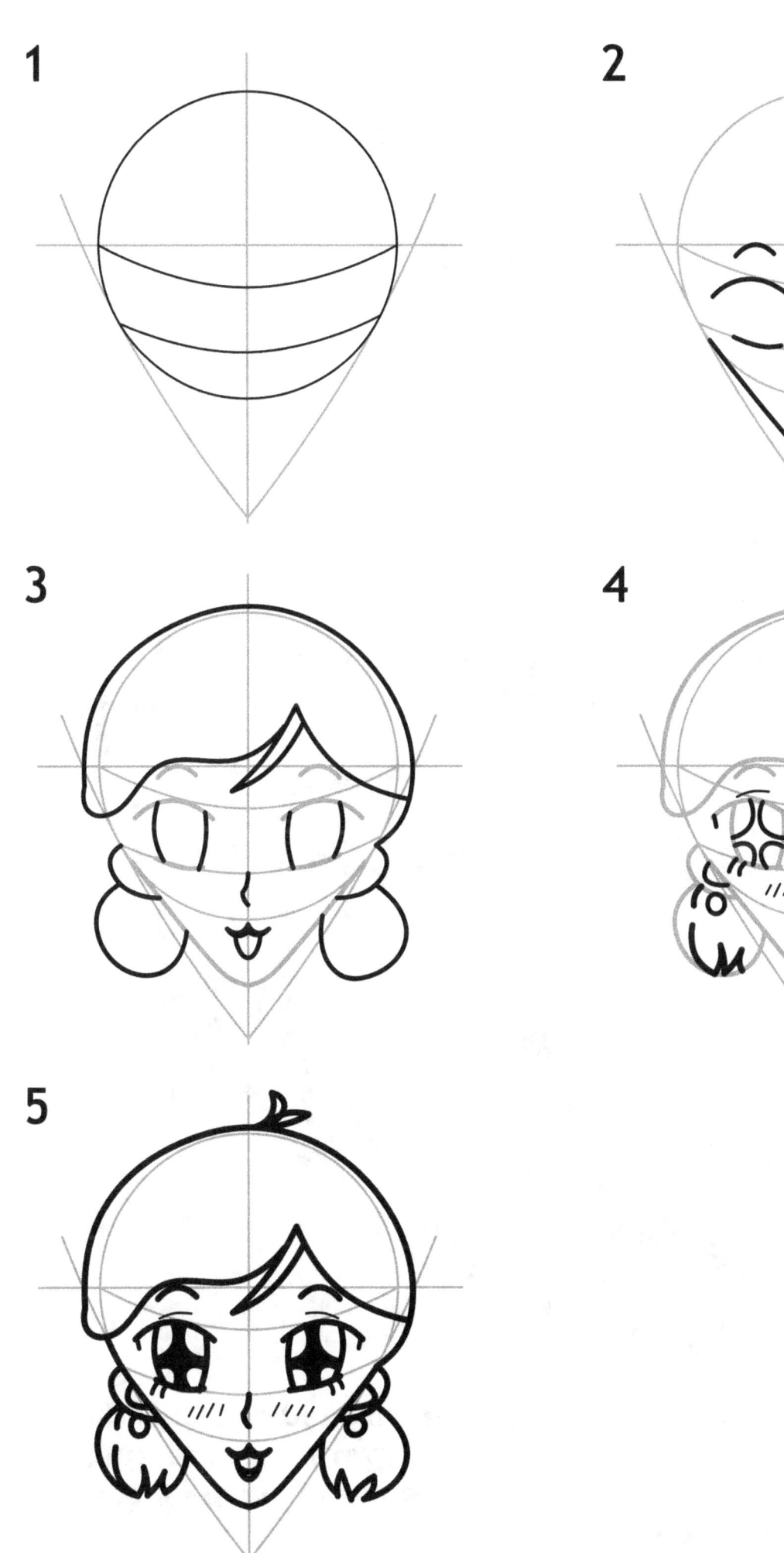

7. Impatient Woman

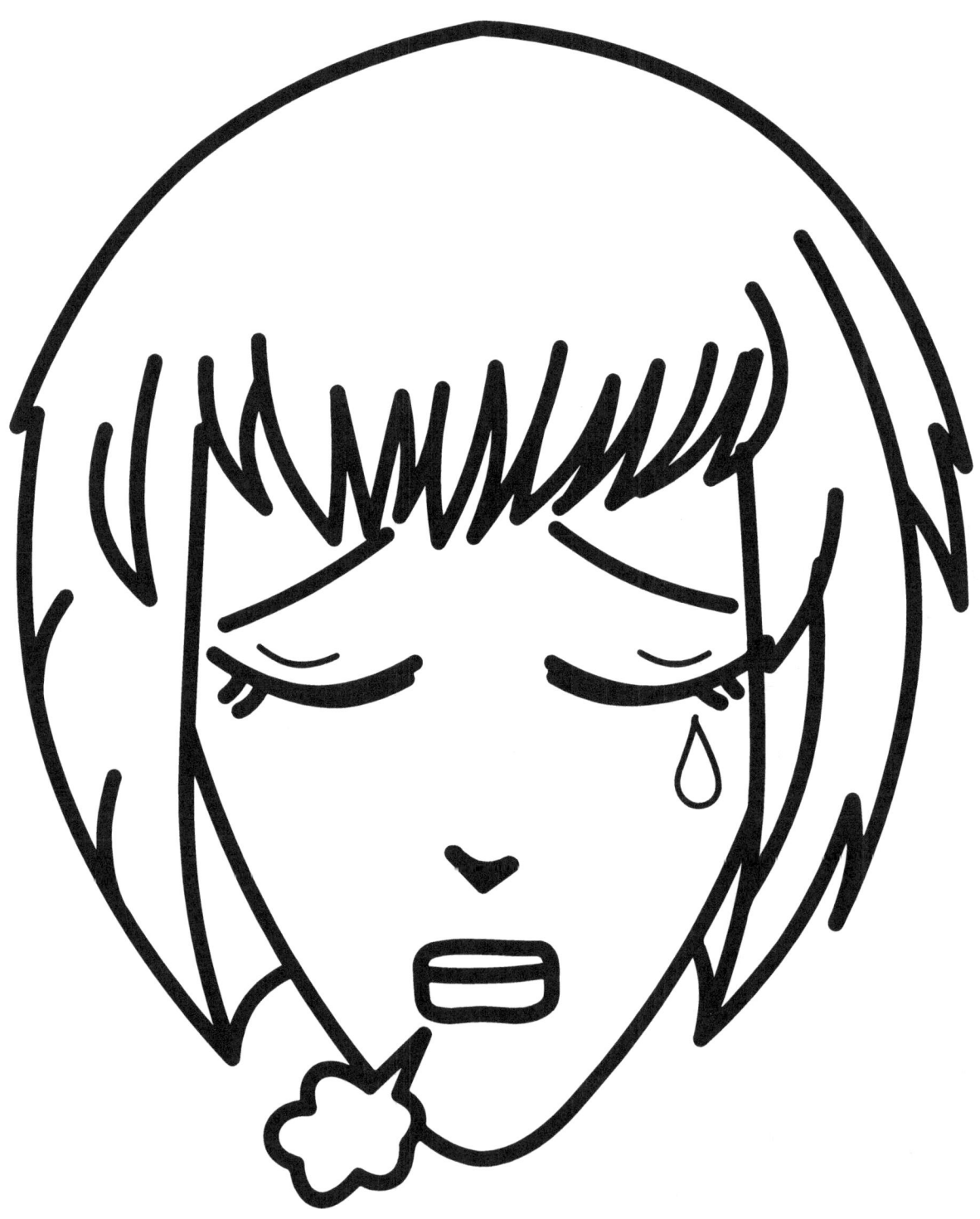

Eyebrows are raised up. Eyes are closed and eyelids are lowered down. A droplet is drawn near one eye. The mouth is slightly opened and a small cloud emerges from it (as exhaled air).

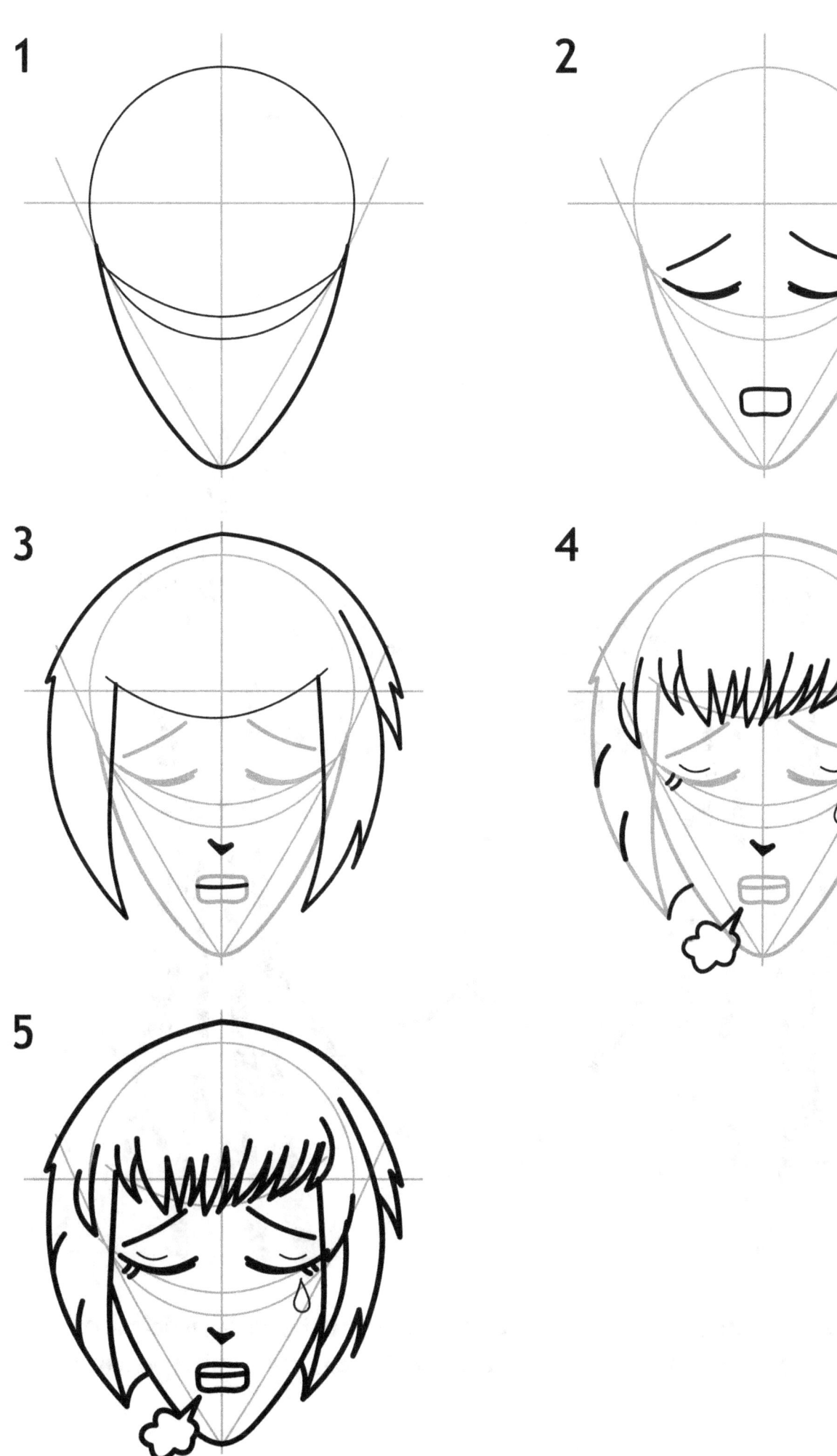

8. Irritated Man

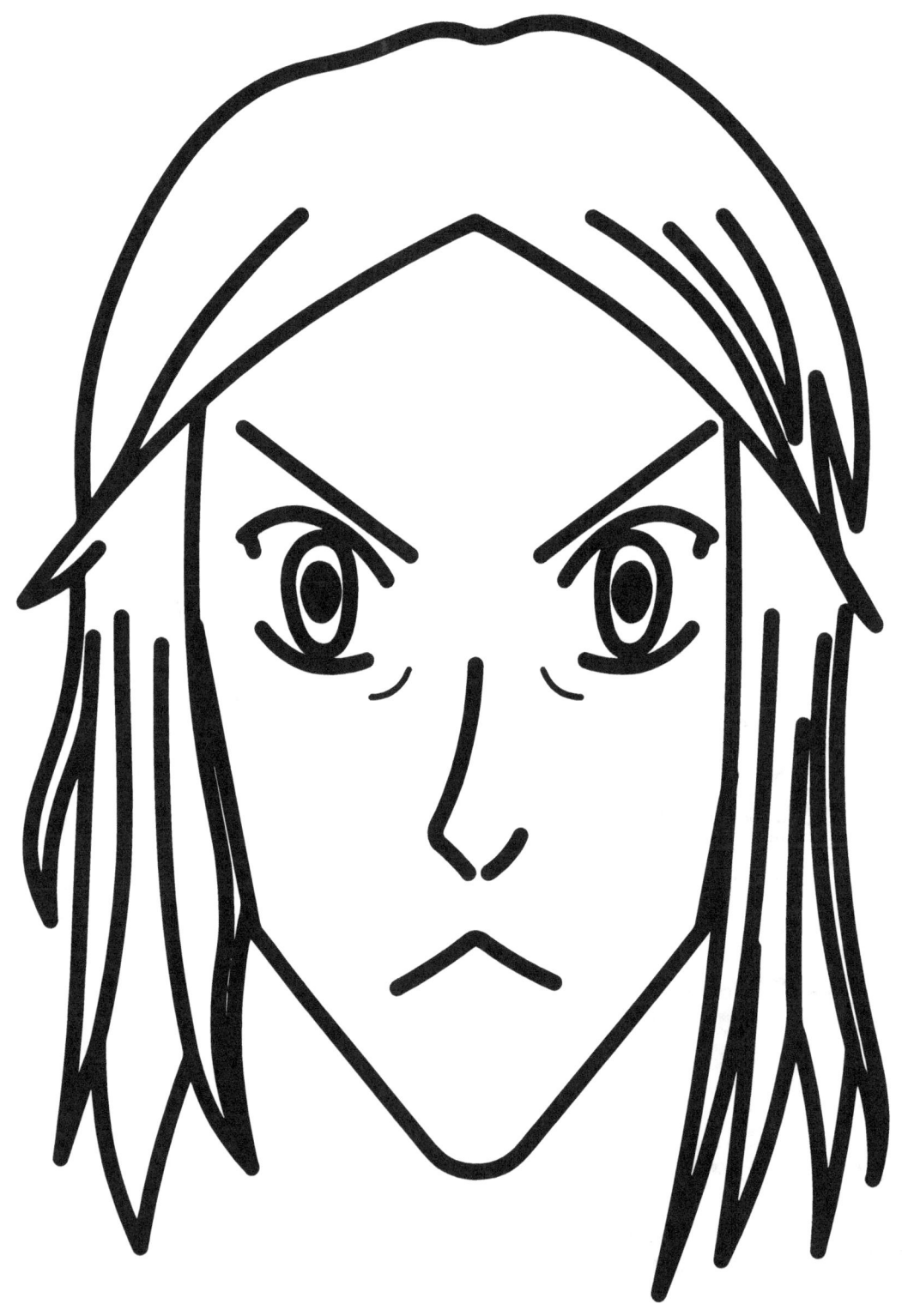

The eyebrows are frowned, lowered to the bridge of the nose. The mouth is curved with an arc-shape upwards.

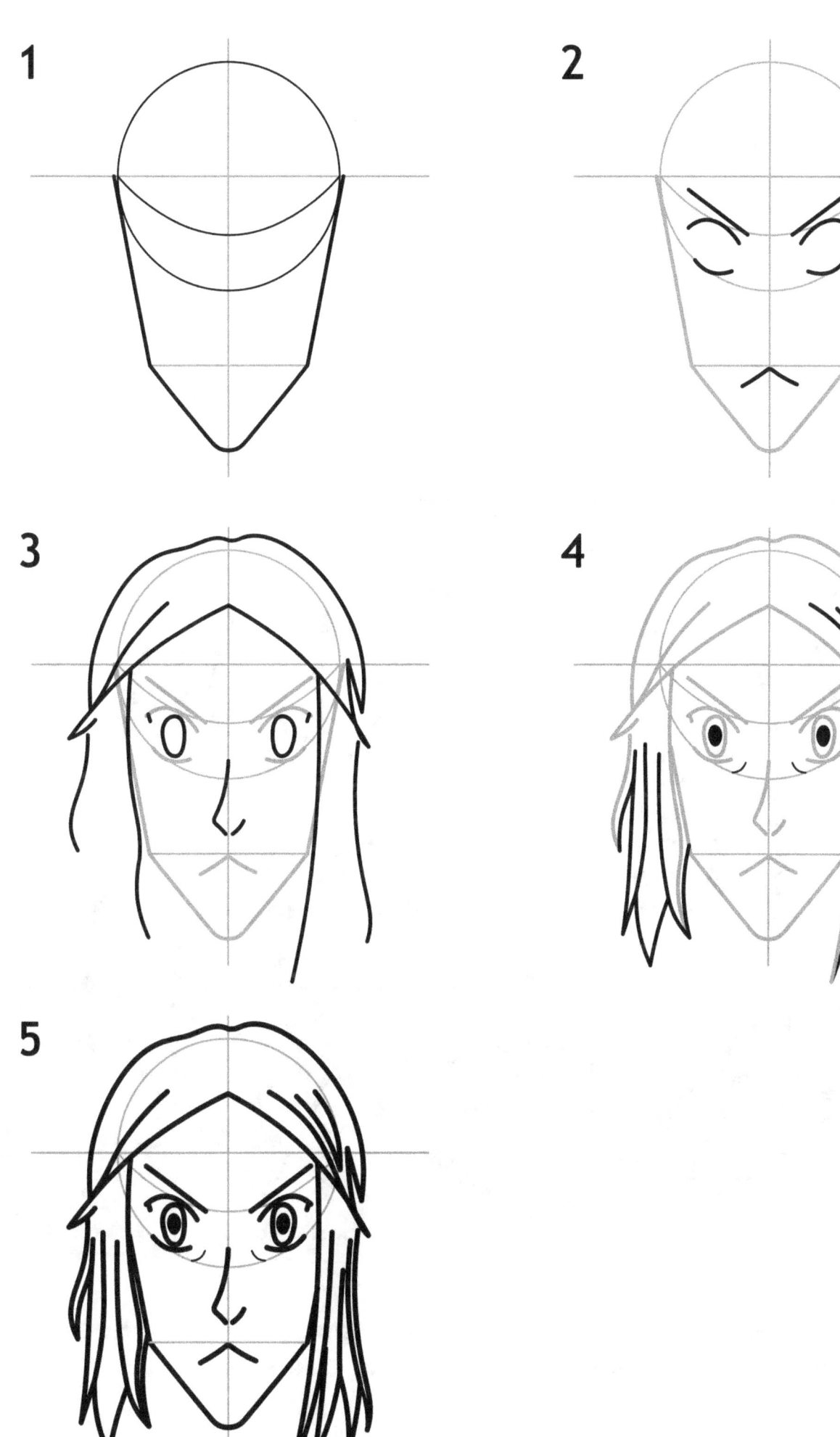

9. Severe Irritated Girl

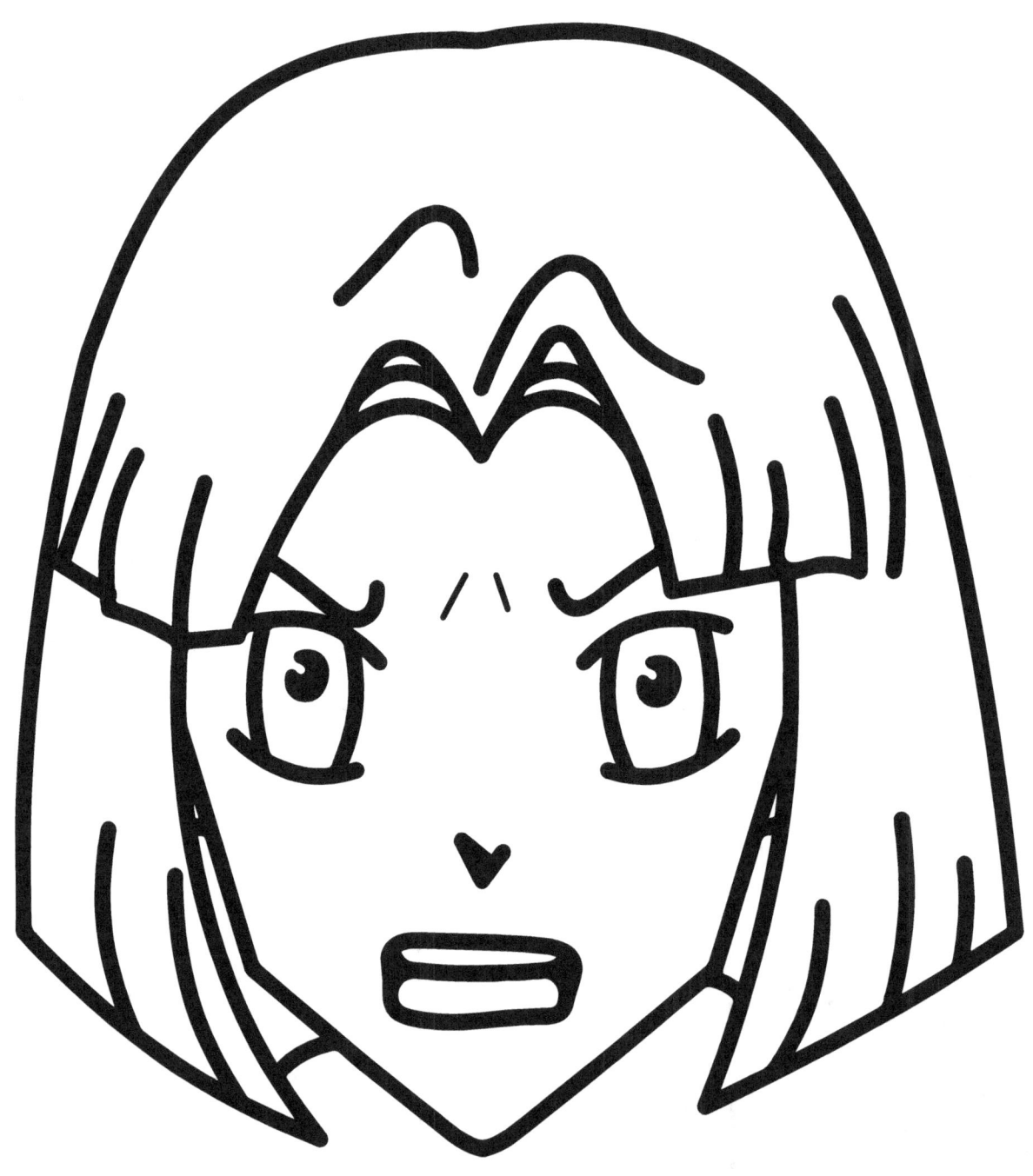

Eyebrows are lowered down and small wrinkles are created between them. The mouth is opened.

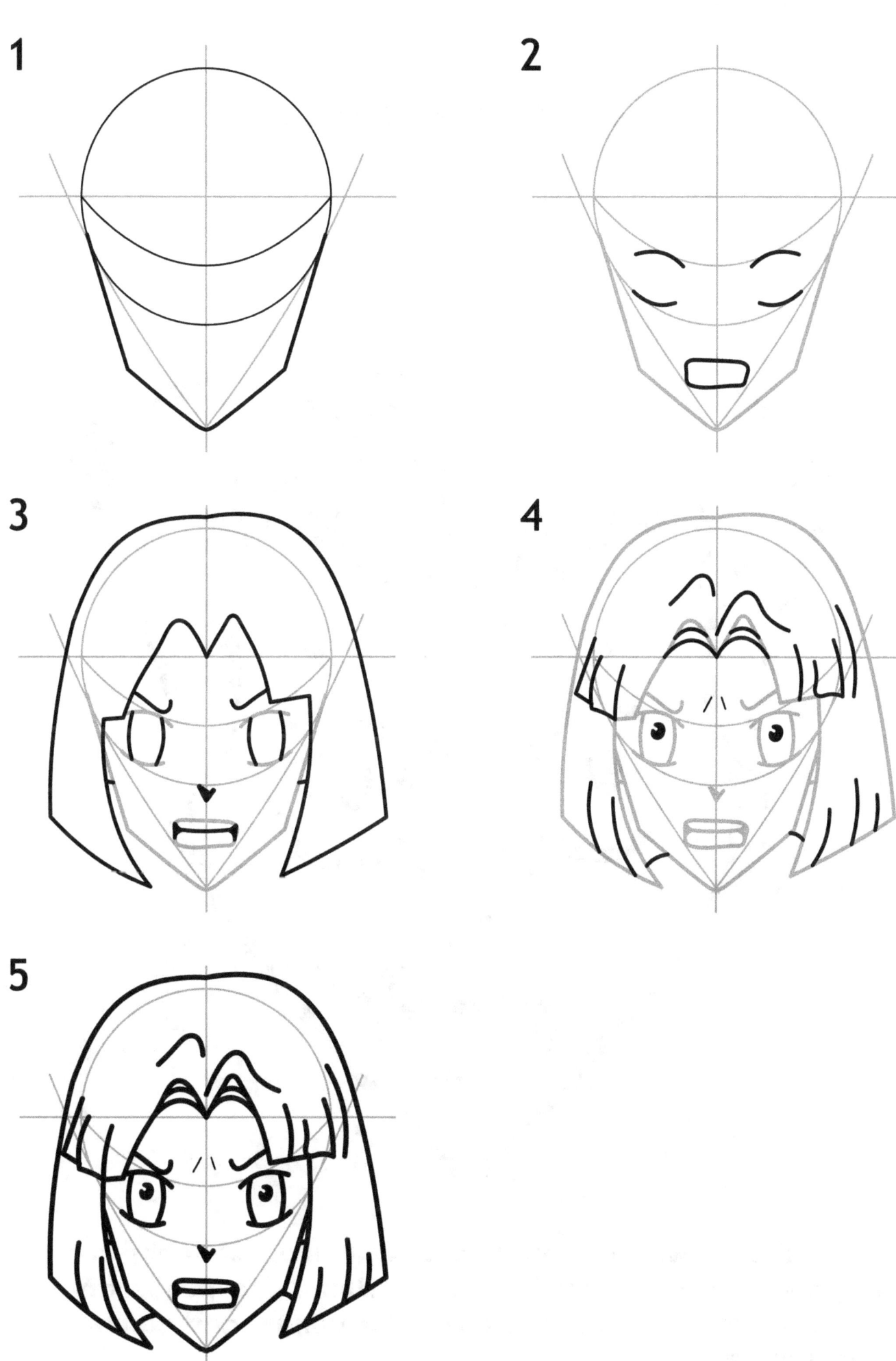

10. Angry Boy

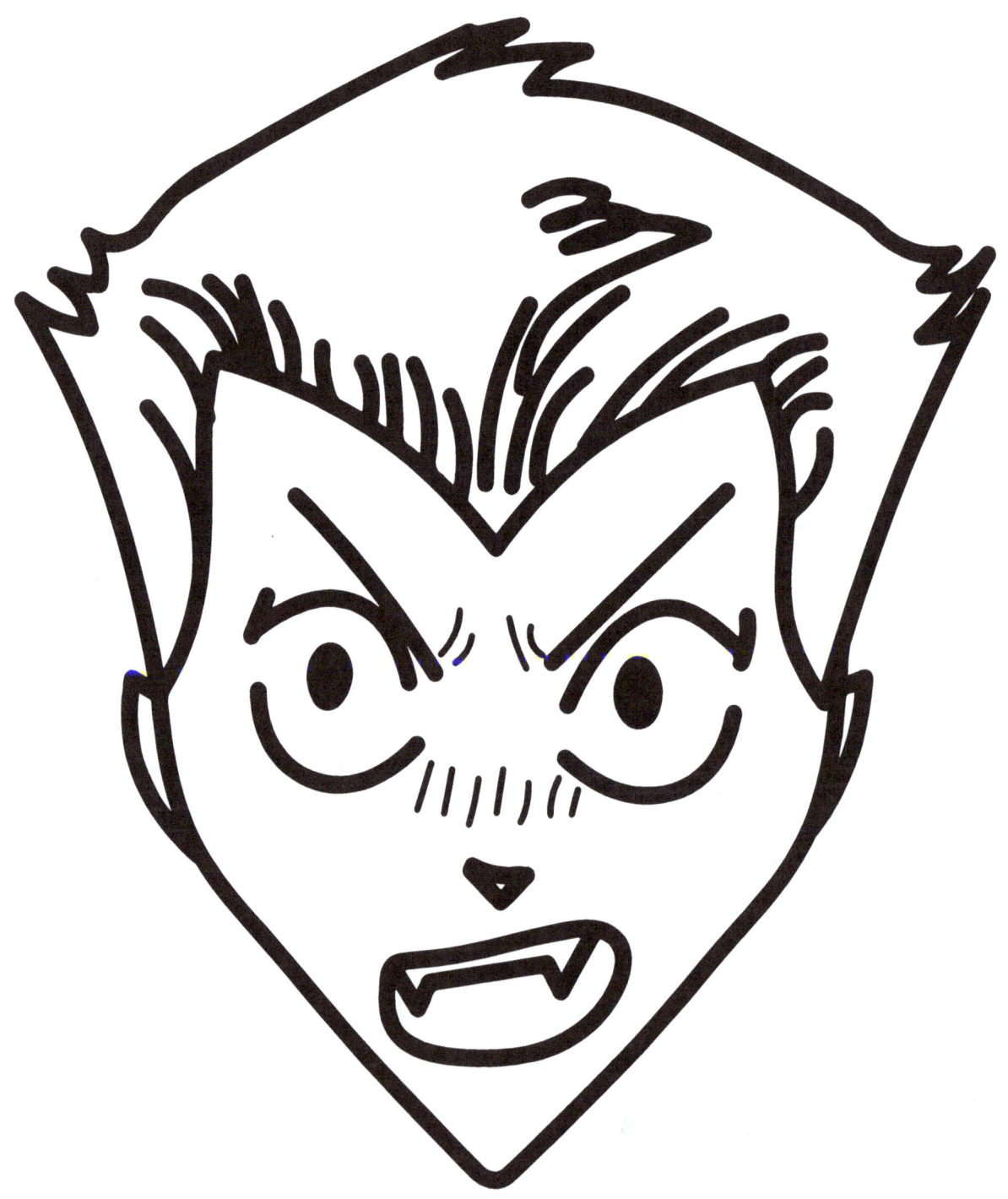

Eyebrows are lowered downwards sharply and wrinkles are created between them. The pupils are narrowed. The mouth is opened strongly and canines are visible.

1

2

3

4

5

11. Girl in a Stupor

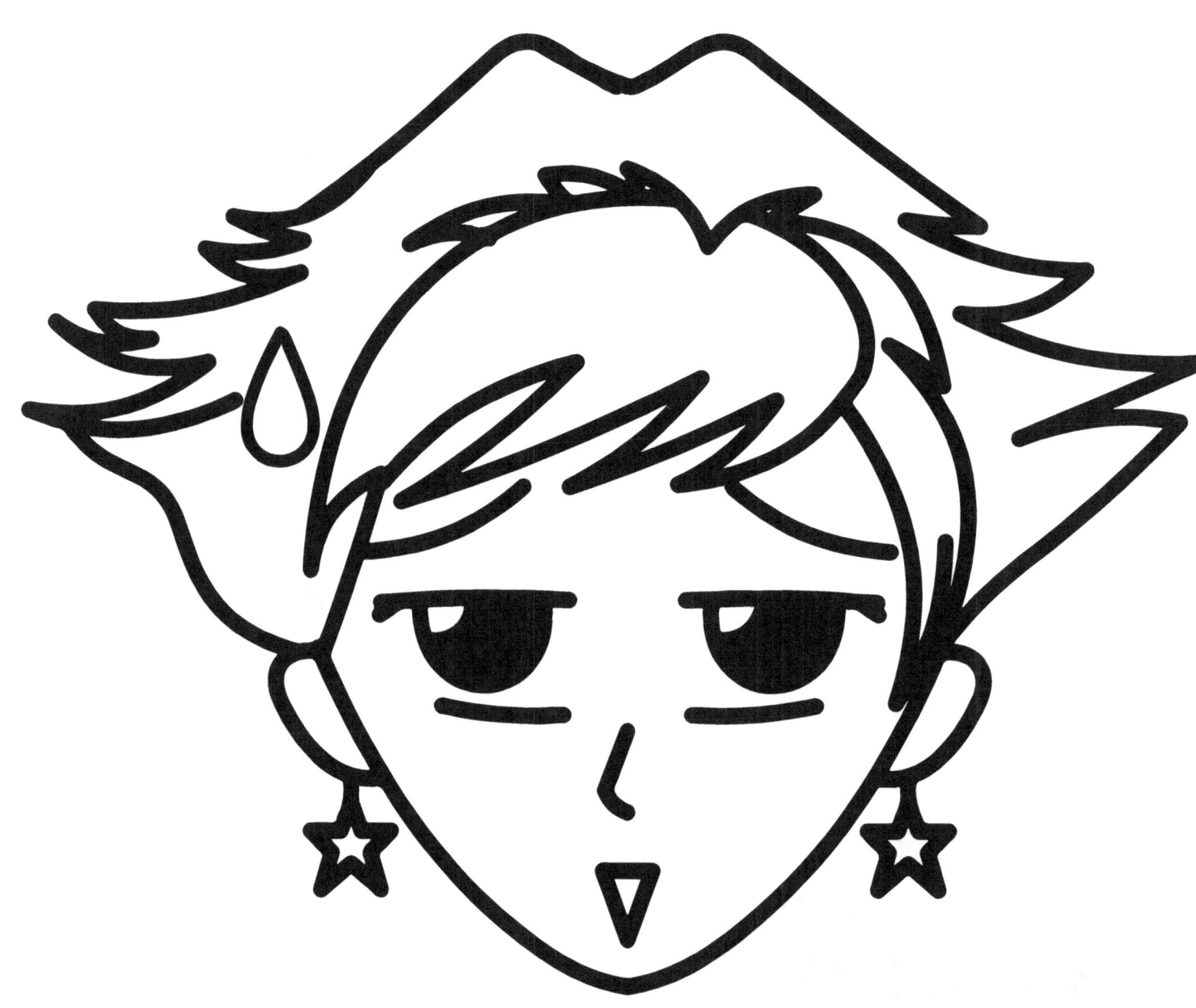

Upper eyelids are straight lines. The ends of the eyebrows are raised. The pupils of the eyes are large without the iris of the eye. Mouth is in the form of a triangle. Droplet is drawn on the side of a face.

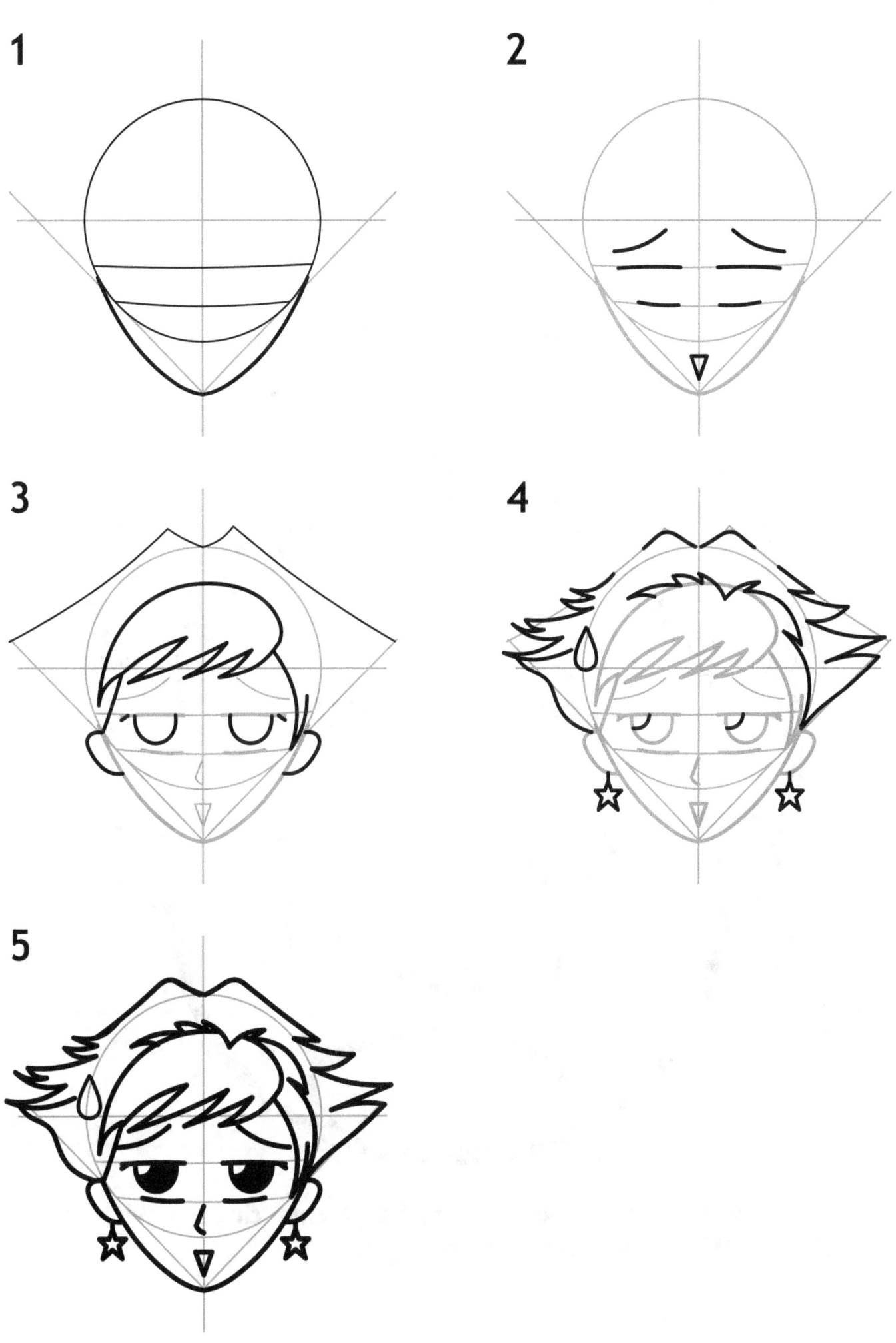

12. Boy in a Strong Stupor

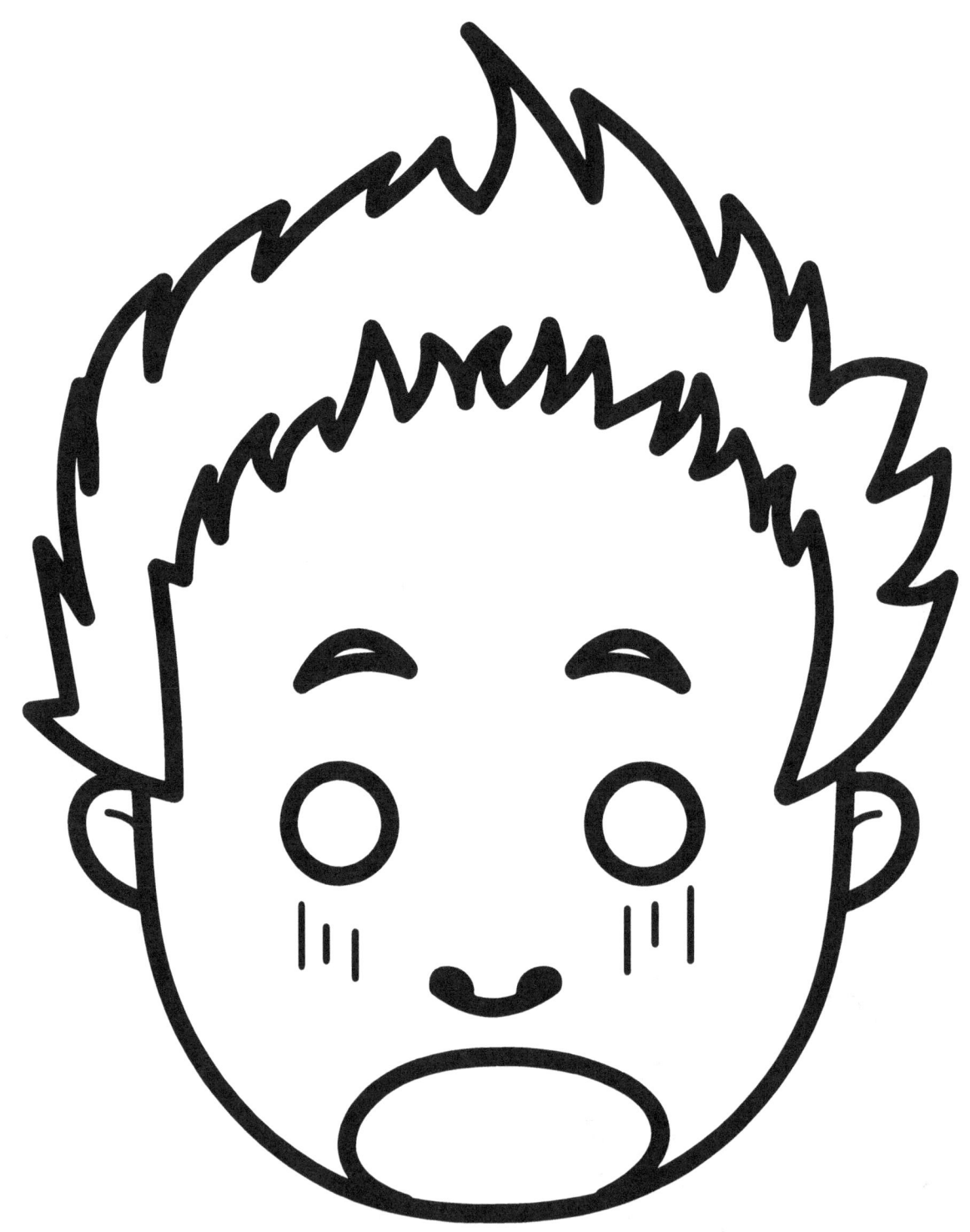

Eyebrows are raised up. Eyes are drawn with a circle. The mouth is open strongly.

1
2
3
4
5

13. Frightened Boy

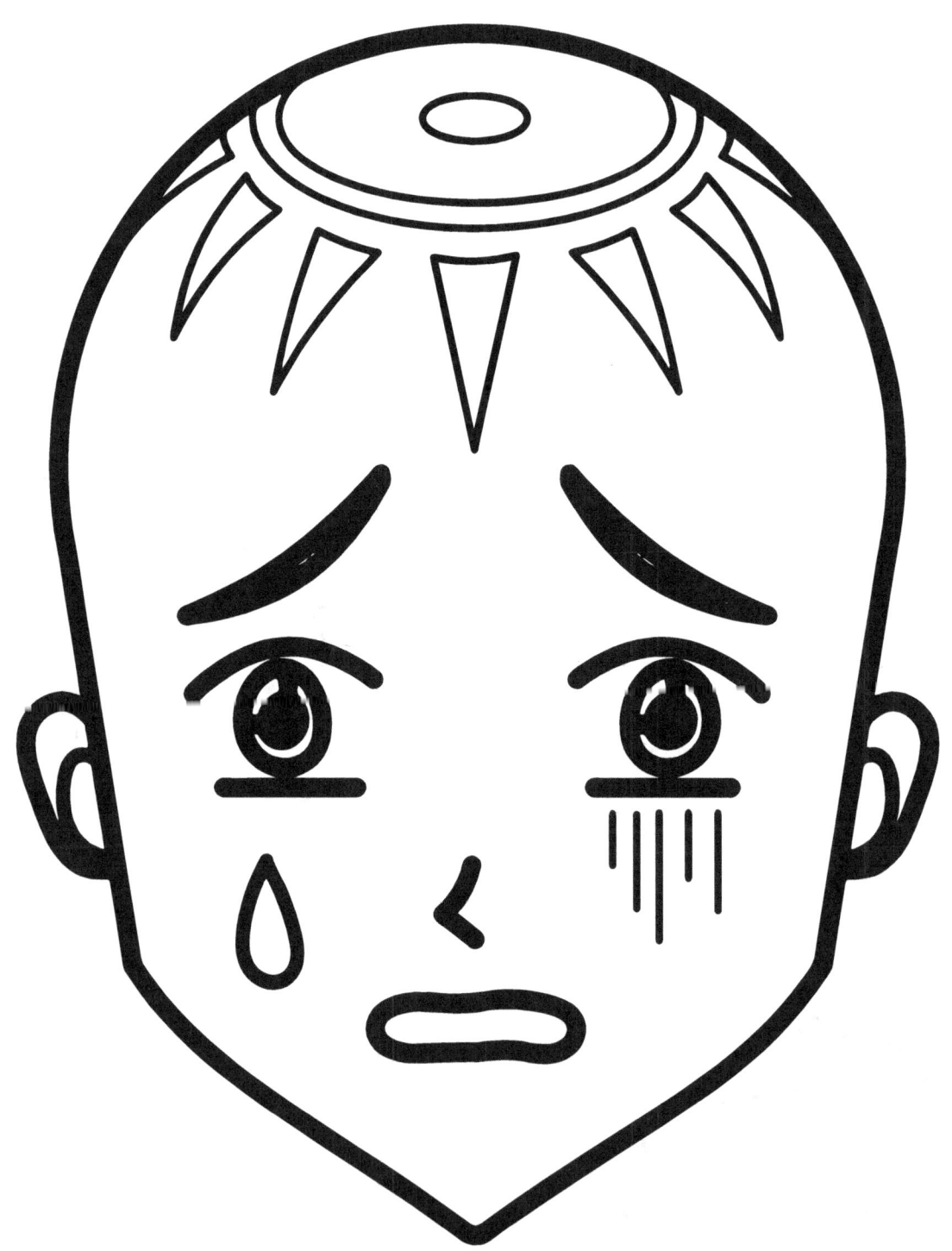

The ends of the eyebrows are raised. The pupils are diminished. The lower eyelid is straight. Mouth is in the form of an uneven oval (as if it is involuntarily opened). There are strokes under the eyes and a drop of sweat.

1

2

3

4

5

14. Disappointed Woman

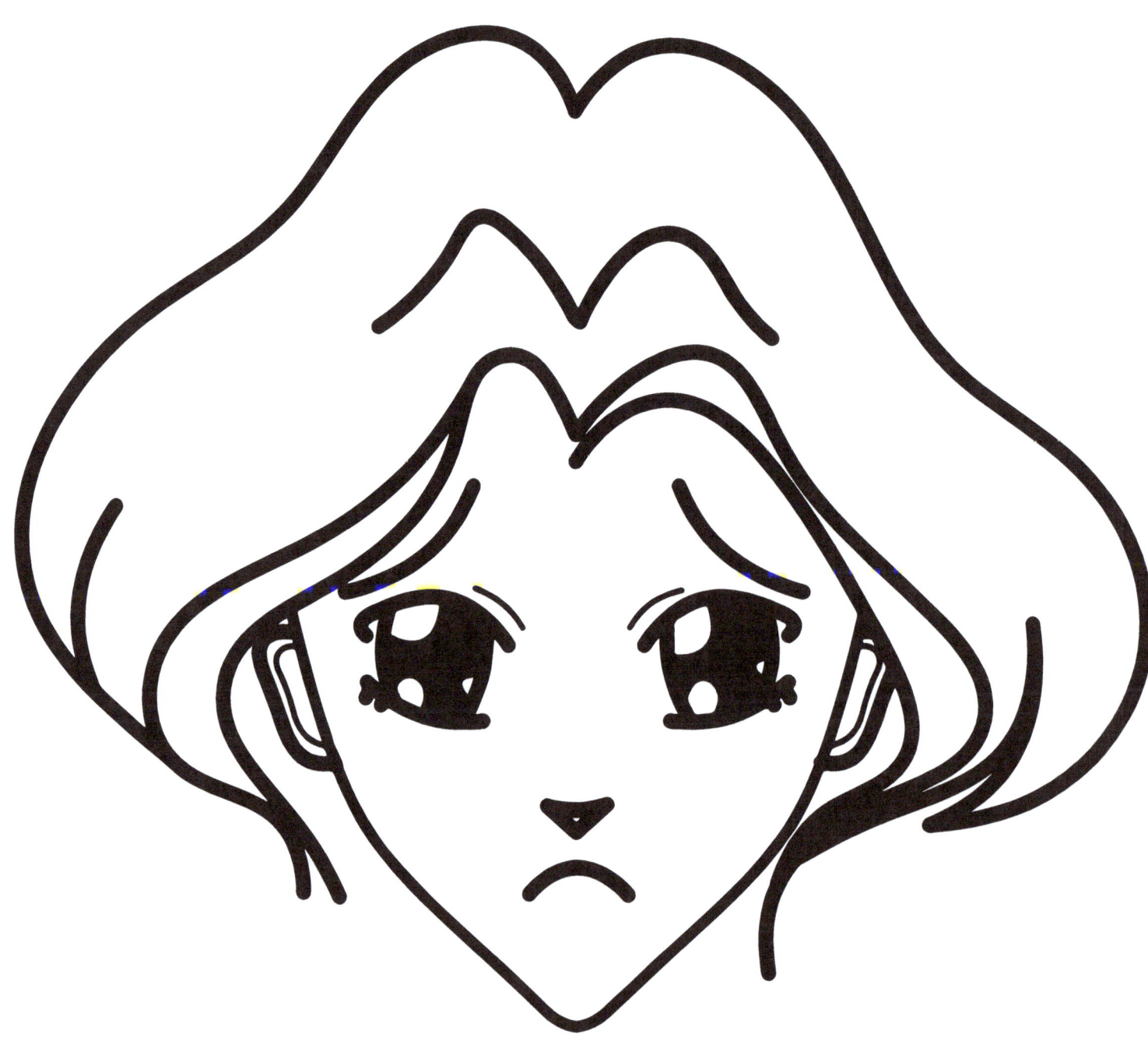

Eyebrows are raised up. Eyes shine with tears. The mouth is arched down.

1

2

3

4

5

15. Crying Girl

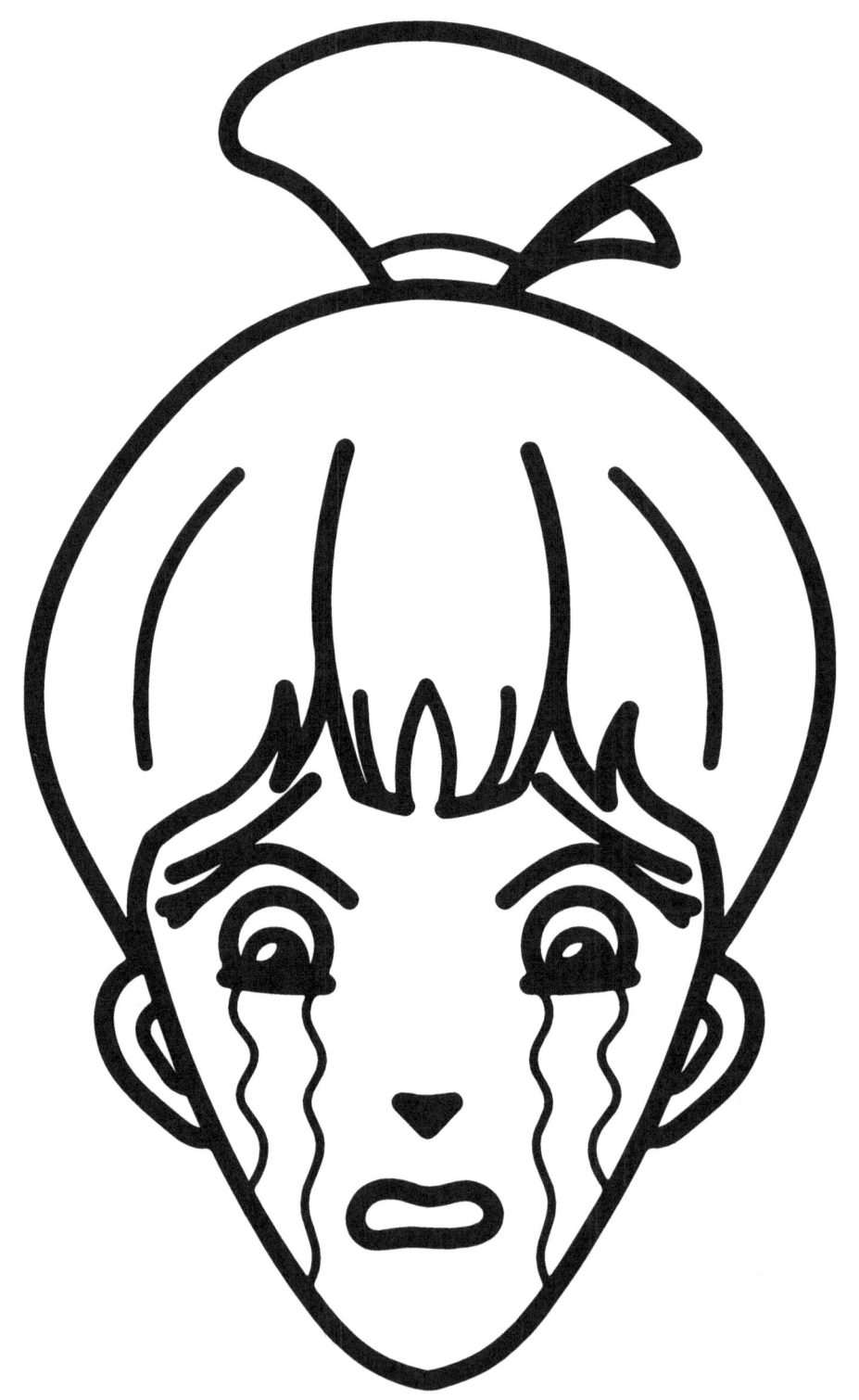

Eyebrows are raised up. Tears come from the eyes. The mouth is slightly opened. Instead the lines of tears, you can also draw droplets.

1

2

3

4

5

16. Weeping Woman

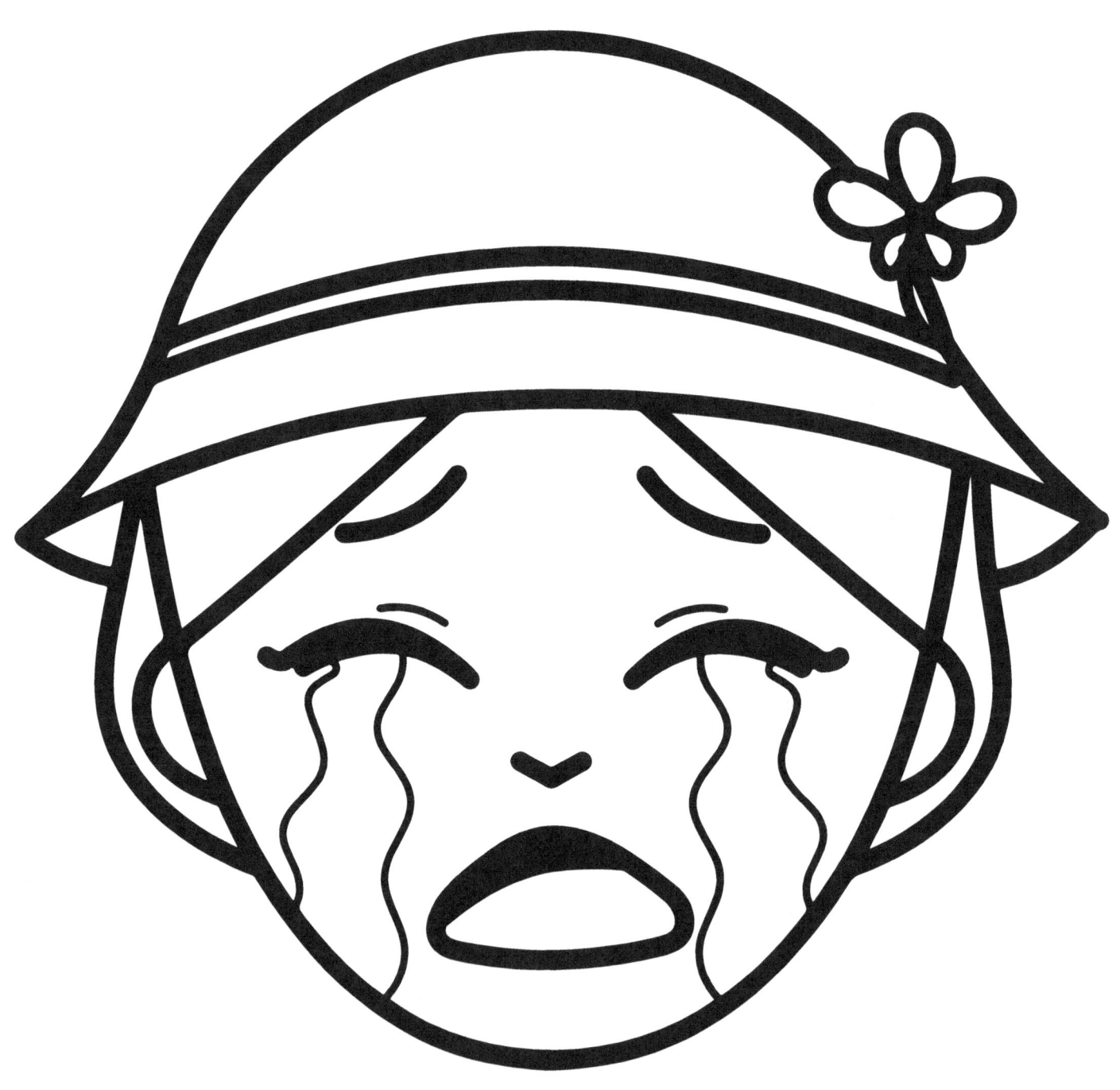

Eyebrows are raised up. Eyes are closed with an eyelid up. The mouth is open widely. Instead of the lines of tears, you can also draw droplets.

1

2

3

4

5

17. Sobbing Teenager

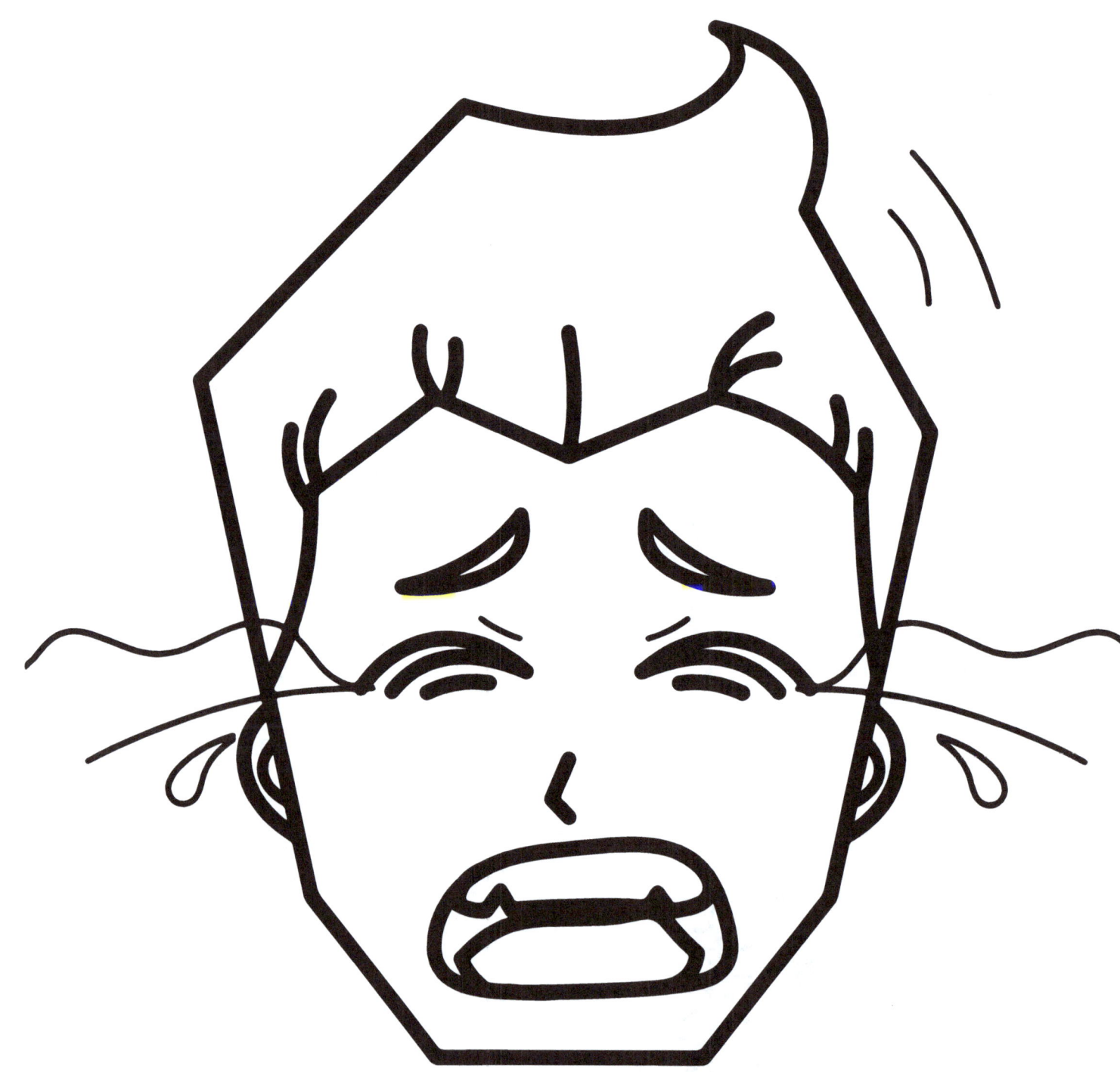

Eyebrows are raised up. Eyes are screwed up with an arc-shape upwards. The mouth is wide opened and canines are visible. There are lines and droplets, going out from the eyes.

1

2

3

4

5

18. Puzzled Girl

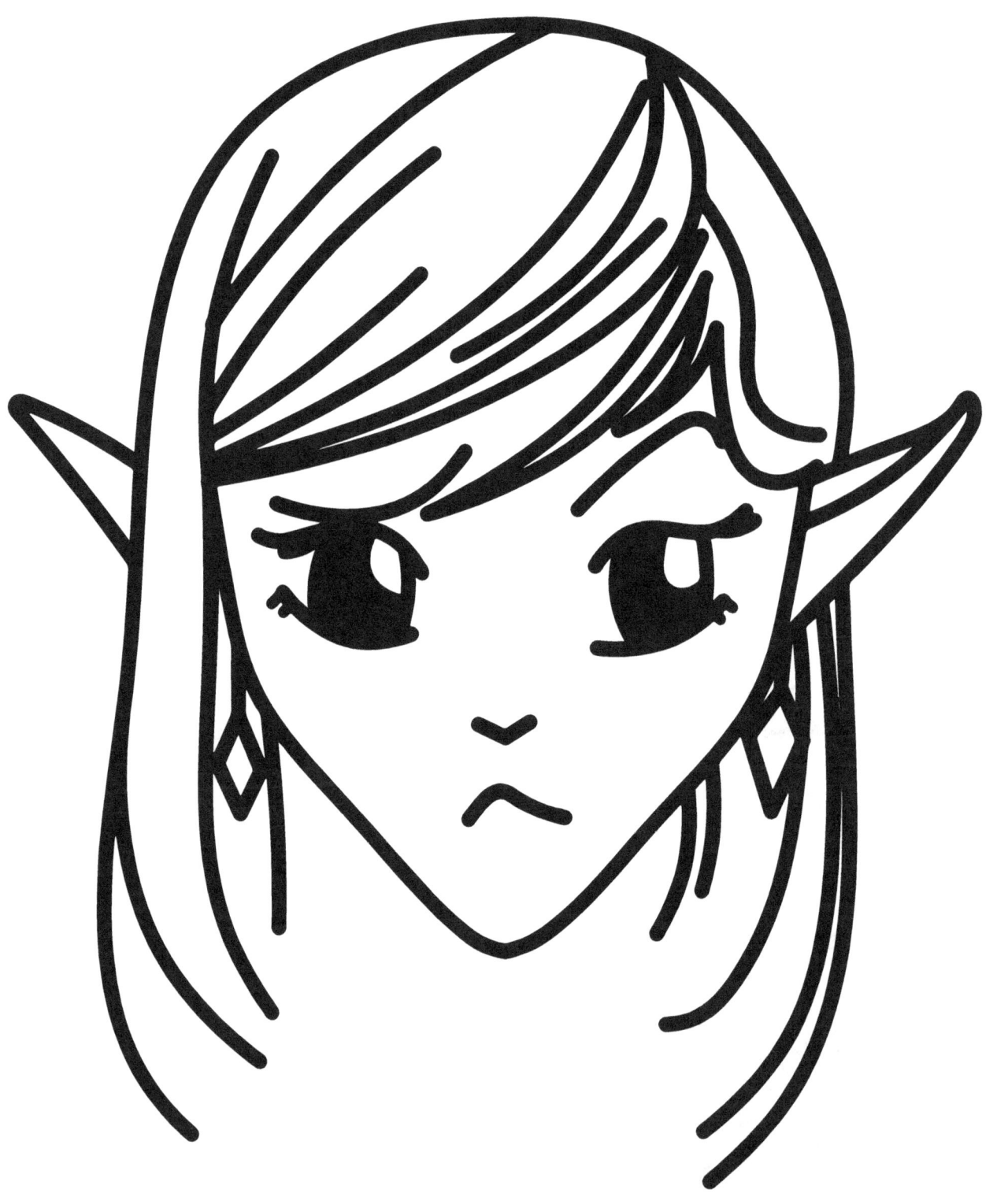

One eyebrow is raised, the other is lowered. Eyes are looking to the side or up. Mouth is in the form of an inverted "V".

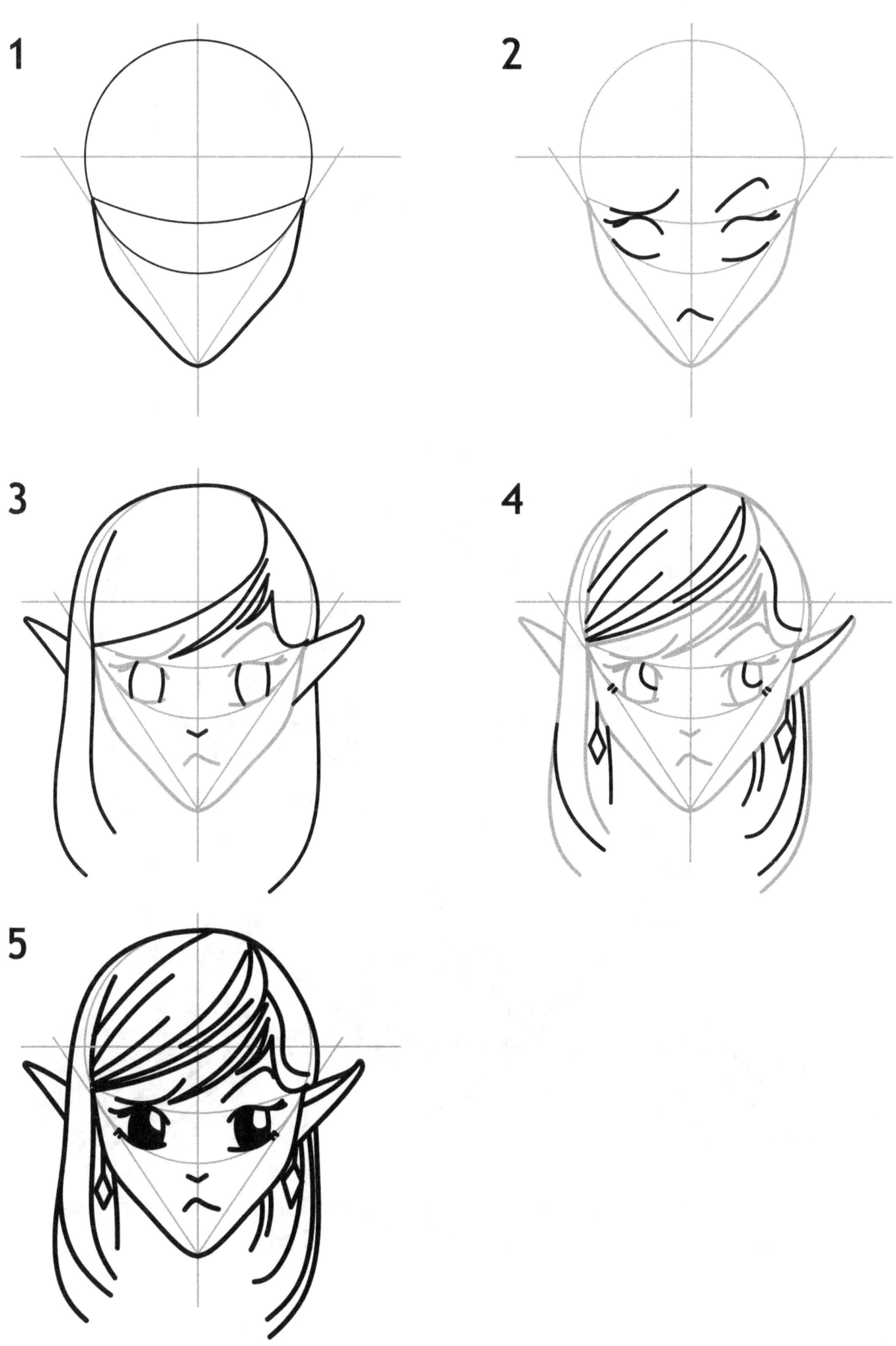

19. Astonished Woman

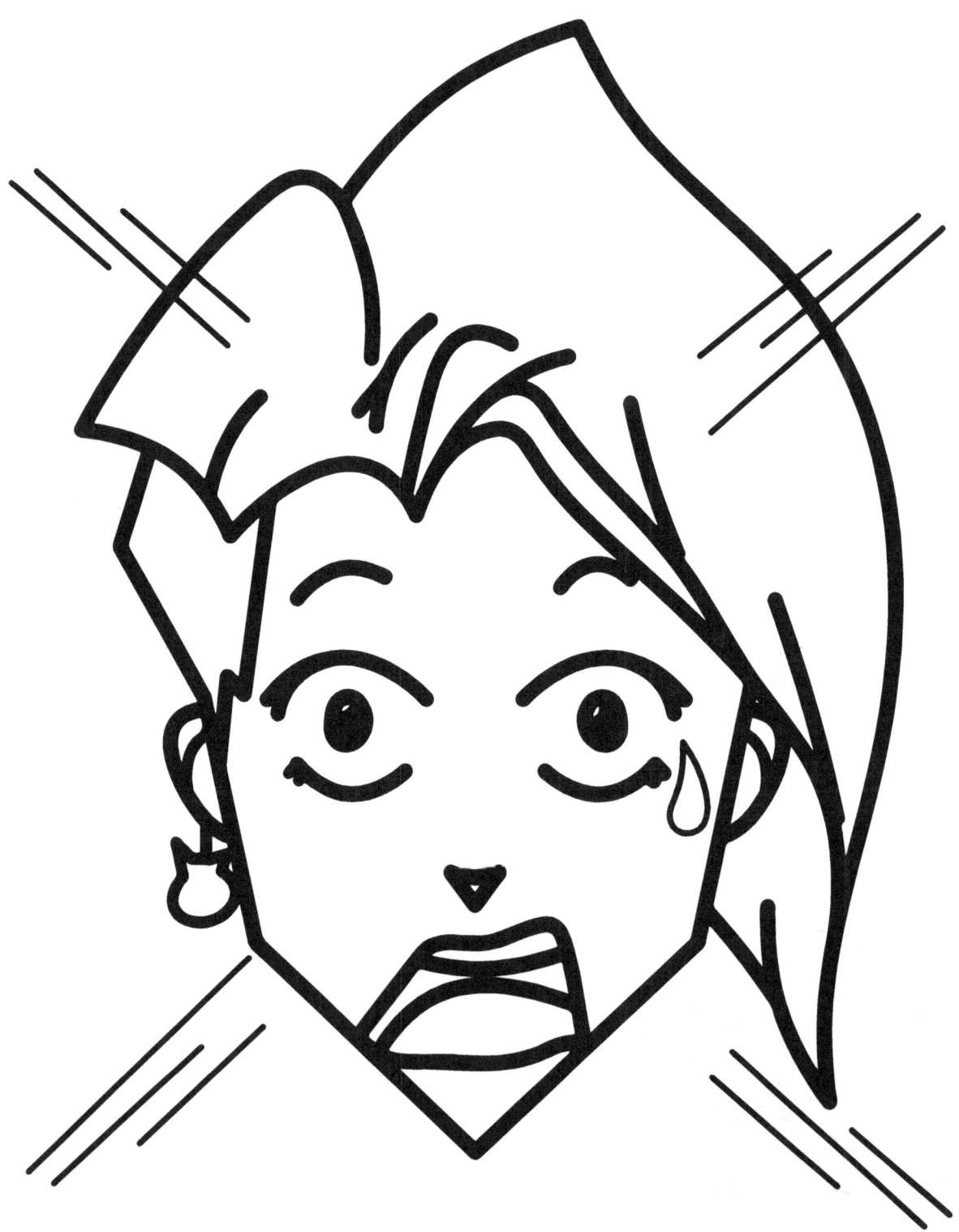

Eyebrows are raised up. The eyes are wide, but the pupils are small. The mouth is opened strongly.

1

2

3

4

5

20. A Greatly Amazed Boy

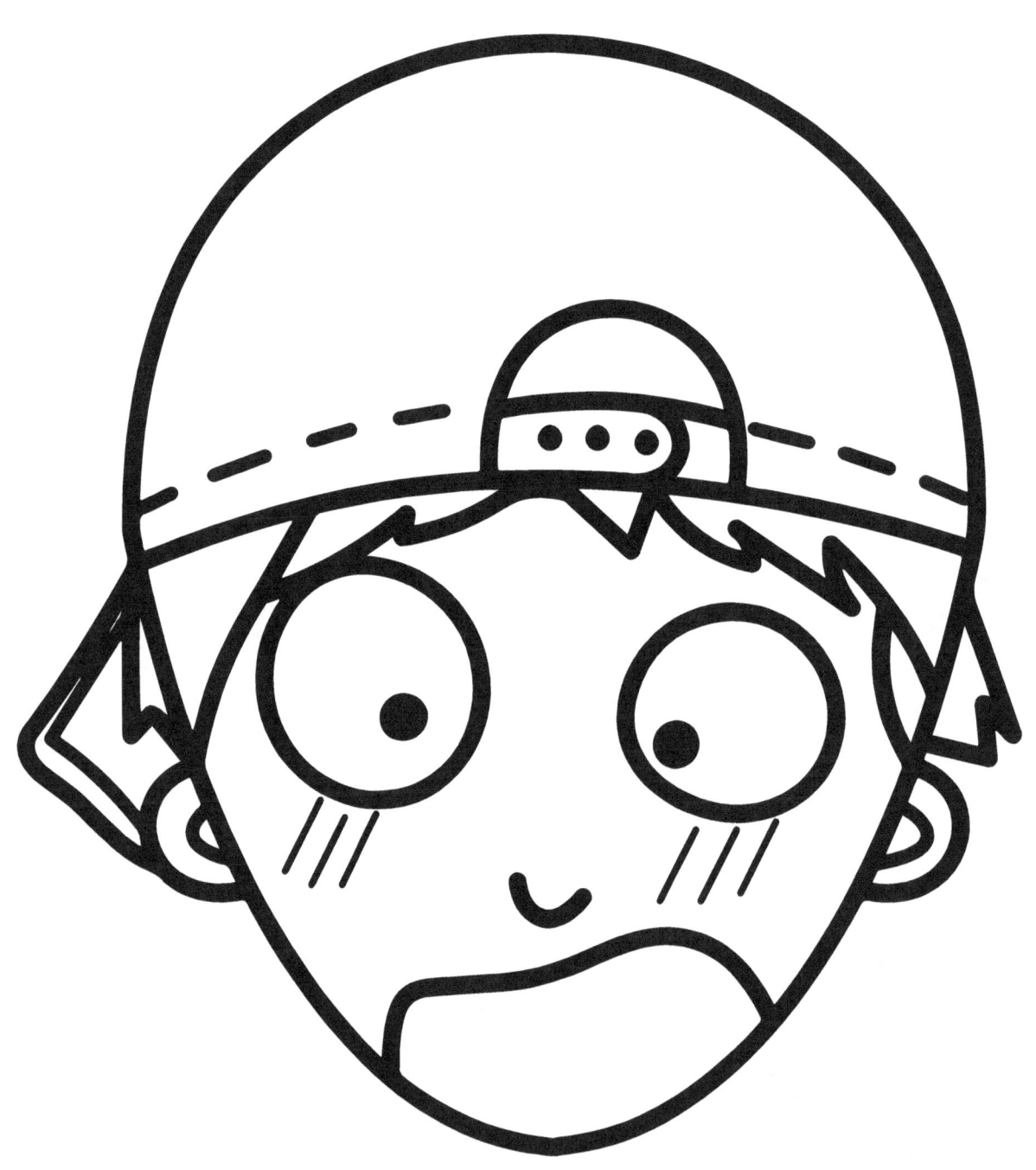

Eyebrows are raised up. The eyes are wide, but the pupils are small. The mouth is opened strongly.

1

2

3

4

5

21. Tired Old Man

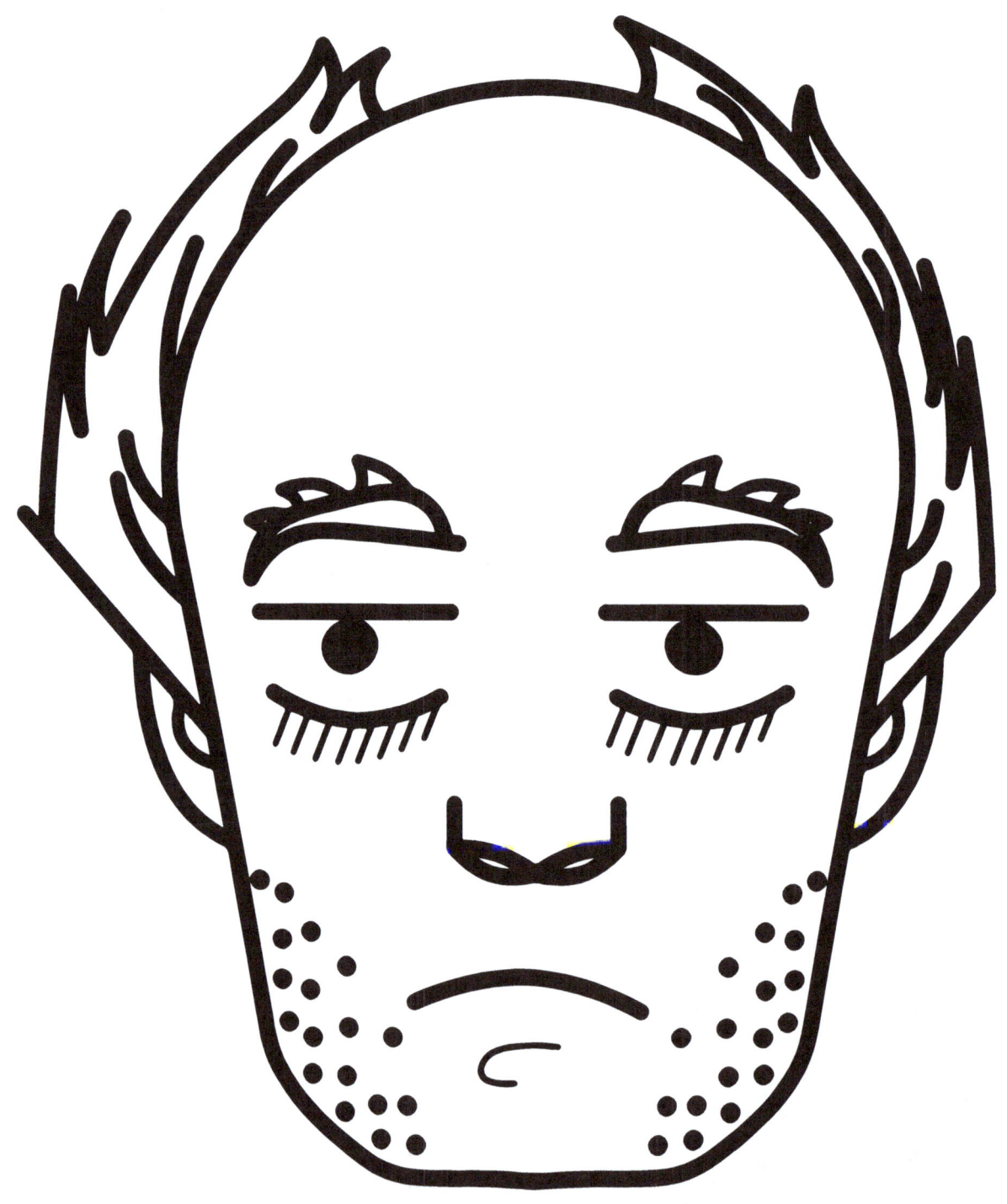

Upper eyelids are in straight lines. Pupils are in the form of dots. There are strokes under the eyes, indicating bruises or pouches. The mouth forms a curved line upwards.

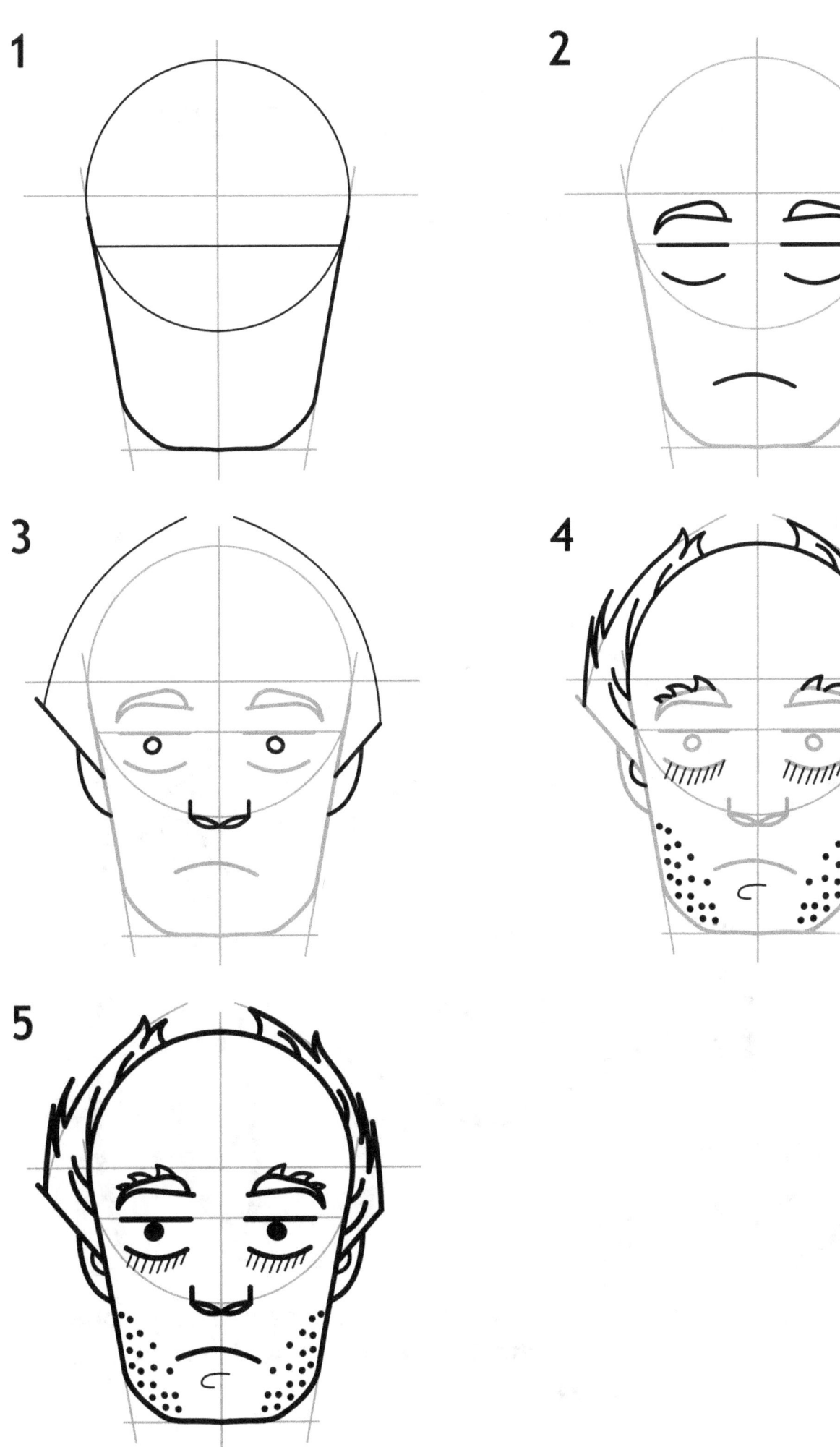

22. A Girl in Disgust

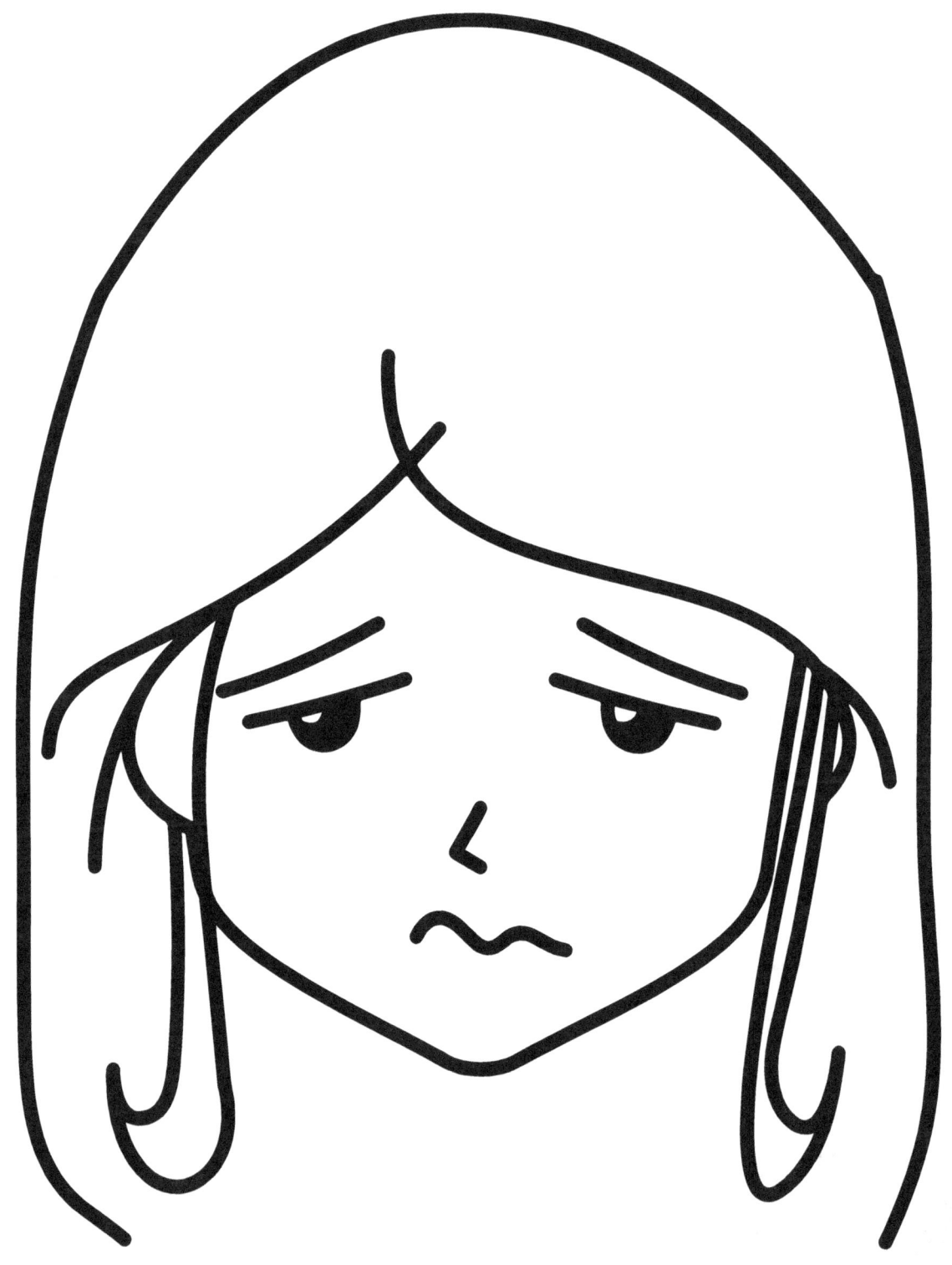

Eyelids and eyebrows are straight lines. The pupils are small. Mouth is at the bottom of the face in the form of an inverted "W".

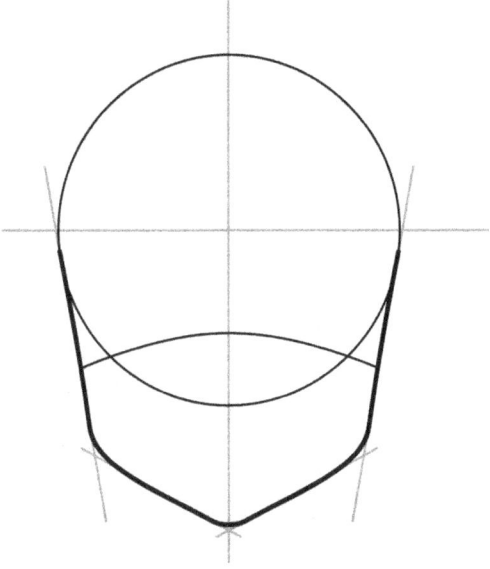
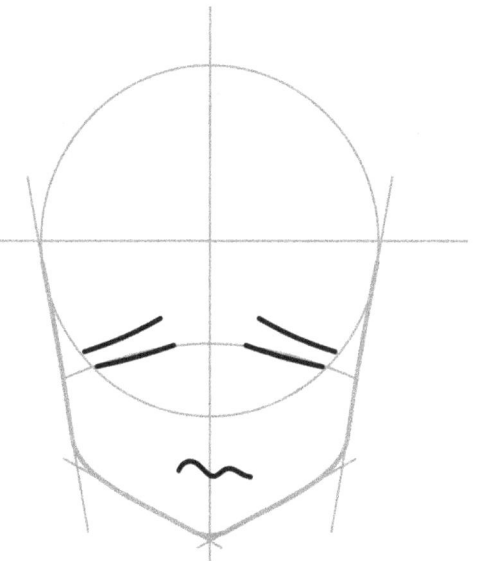
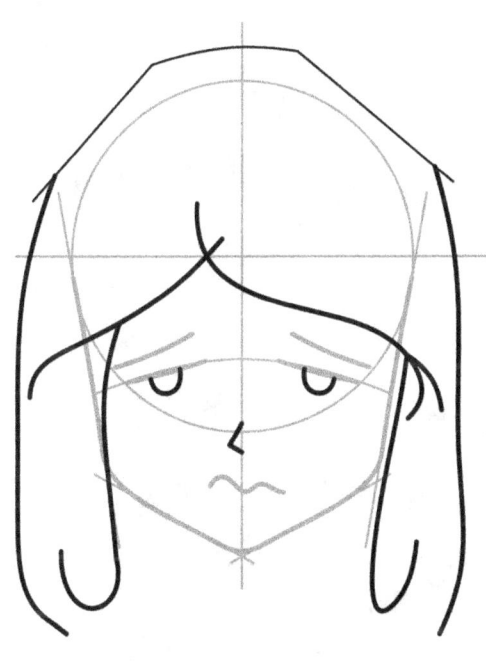
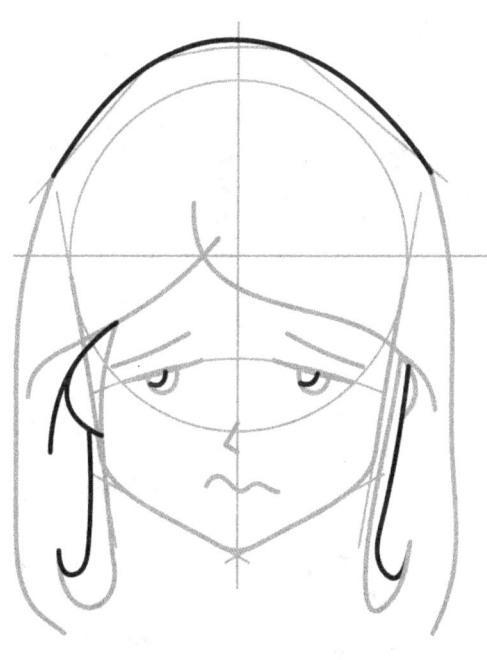
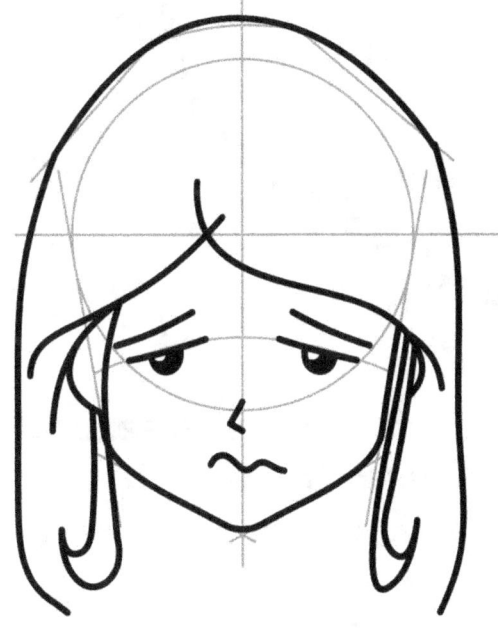

23. A Boy with Tongue Out

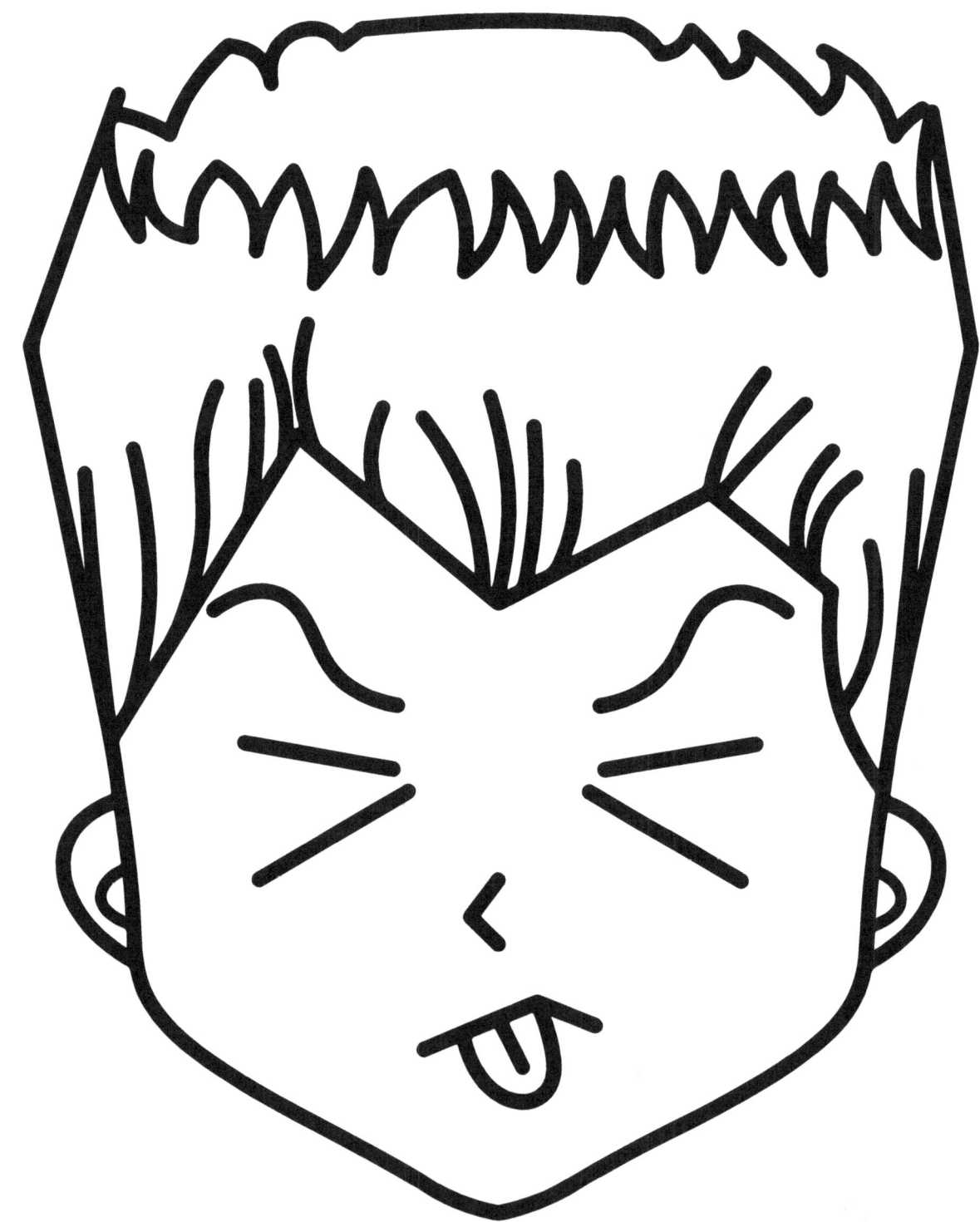

Eyebrows form arches. Eyes are strongly squeezed, forming two lines, similar to the letters "V". Mouth is in the form of an arc with the tongue shown out.

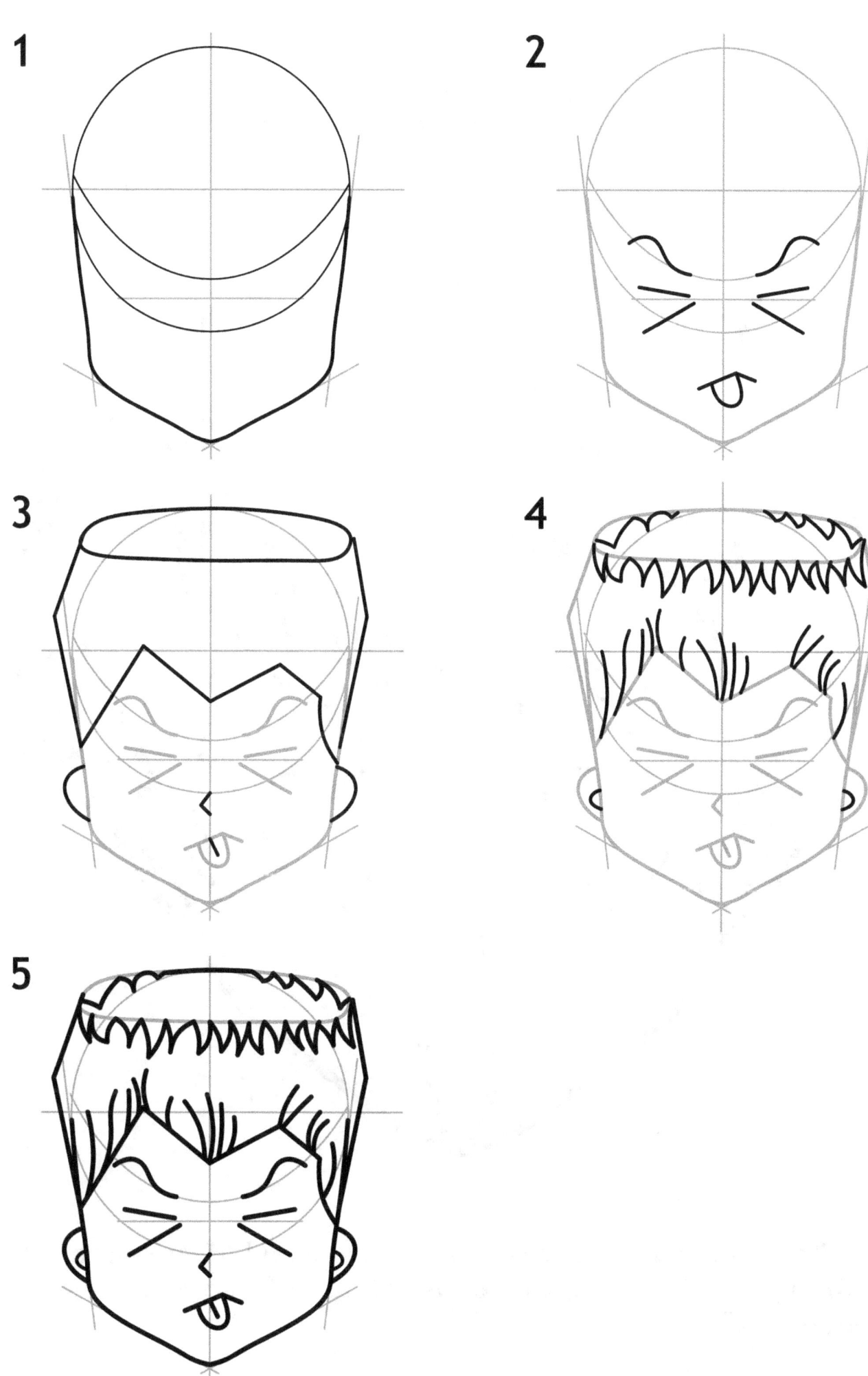

24. Girl in Love

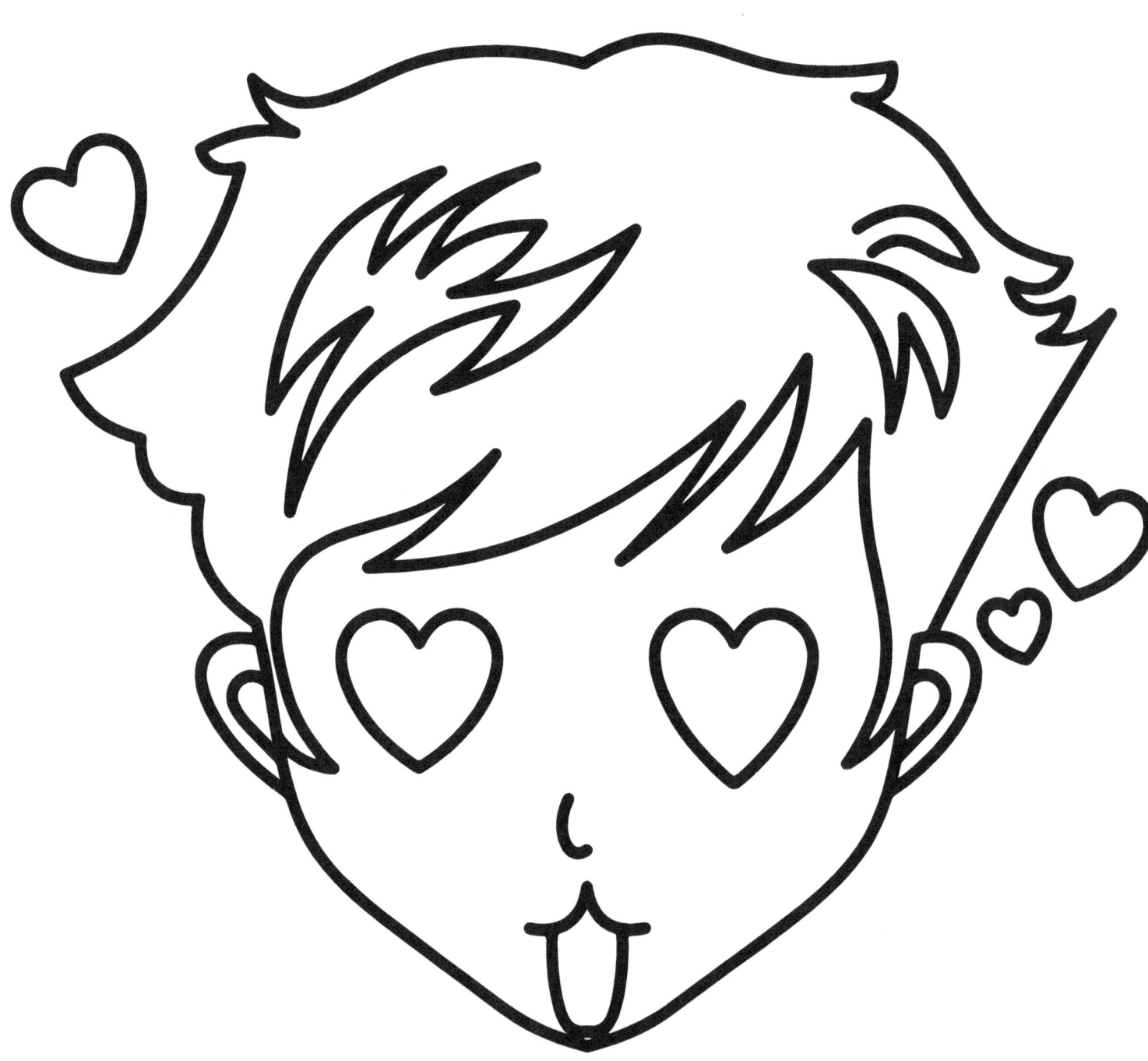

No eyebrows. There are hearts instead of the eyes. The upper lip is similar to the shape of the inverted letter "Z".

1

2

3

4

5

25. Sleeping Woman

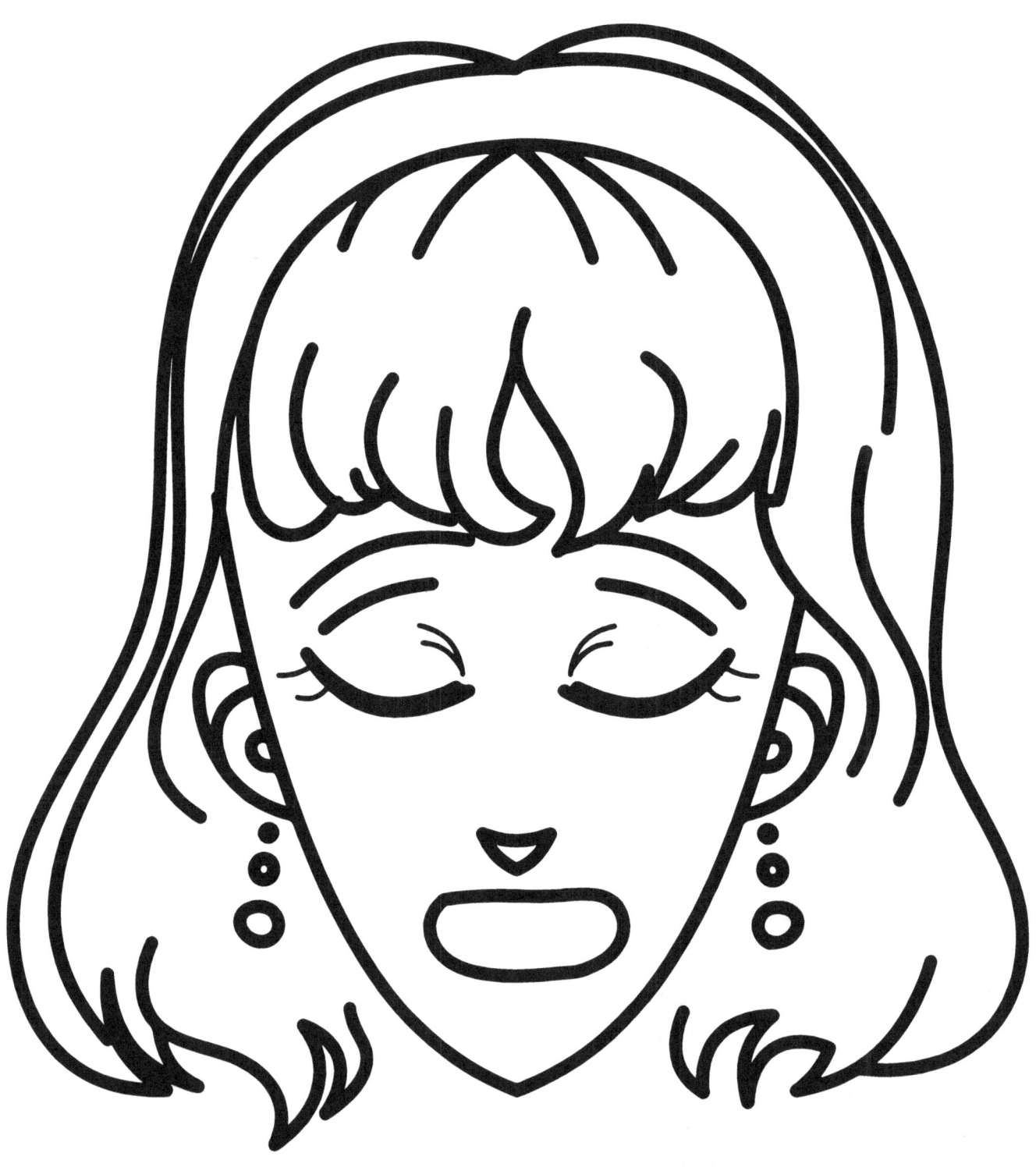

Eyebrows are slightly raised. Eyes are closed and eyelid is down. The mouth is opened.

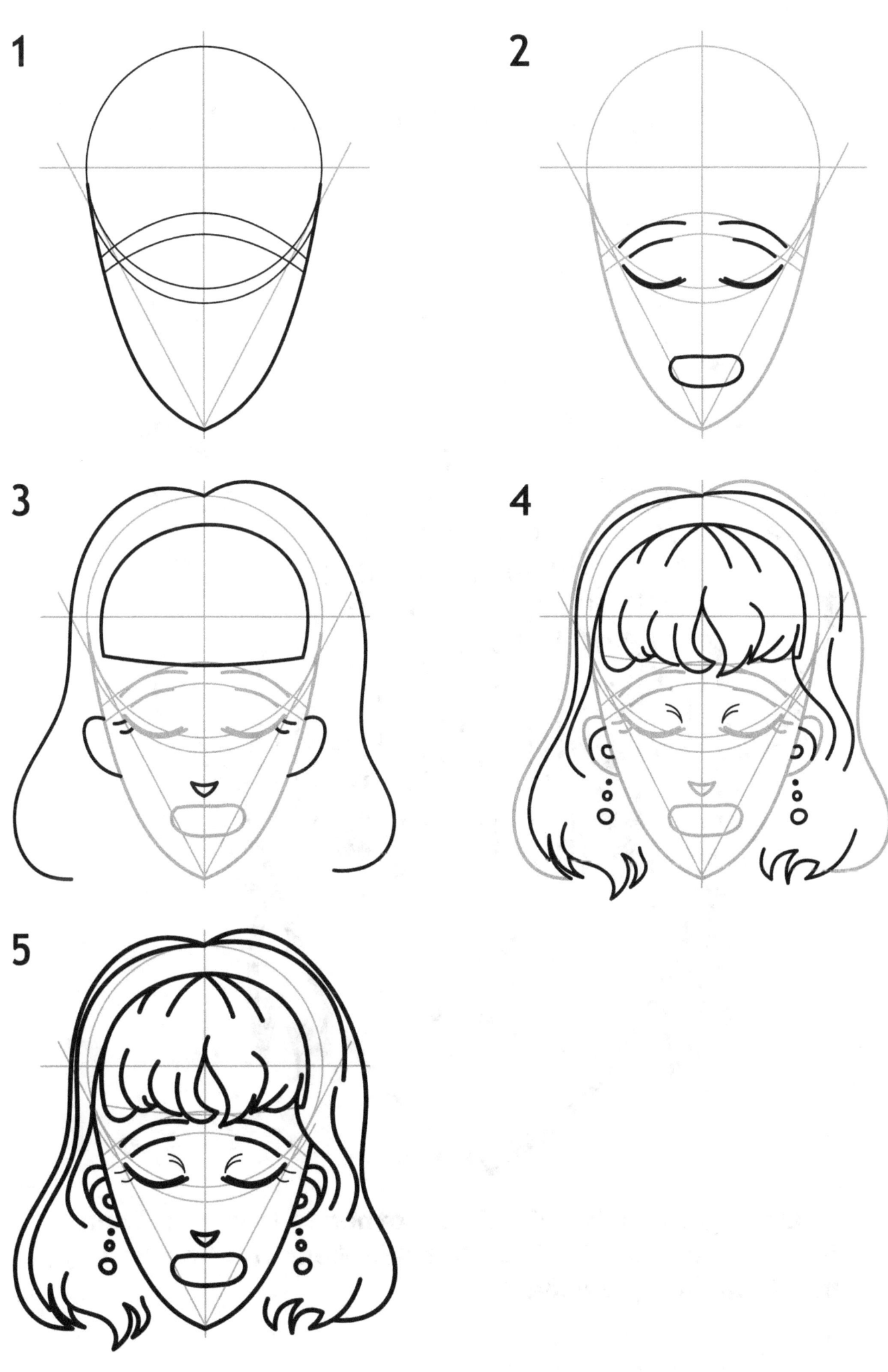

26. Angry and Puzzled Boy

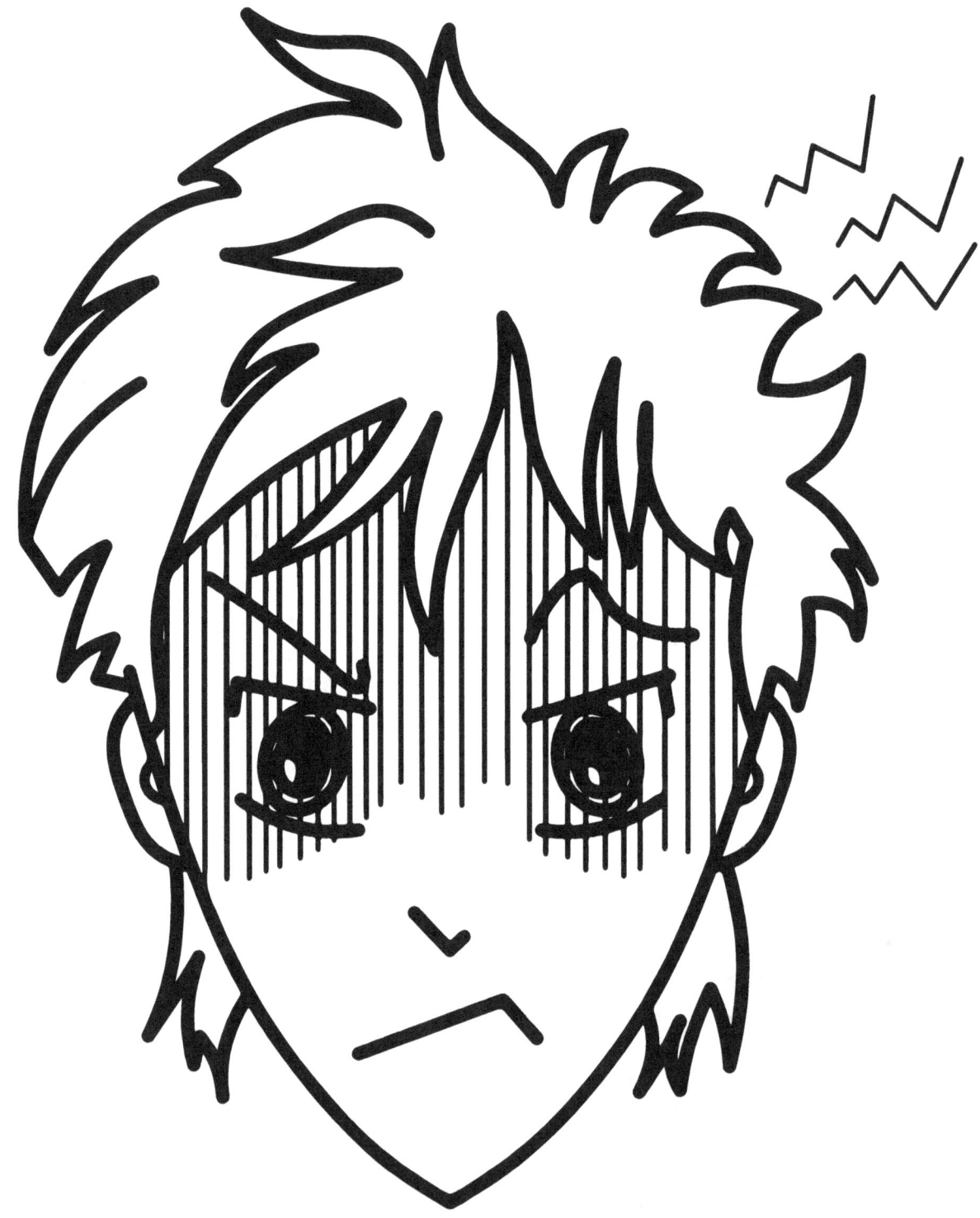

One eyebrow is raised, the other is lowered. There is a shadow on the face like strokes. The line of the mouth is sharply raised.

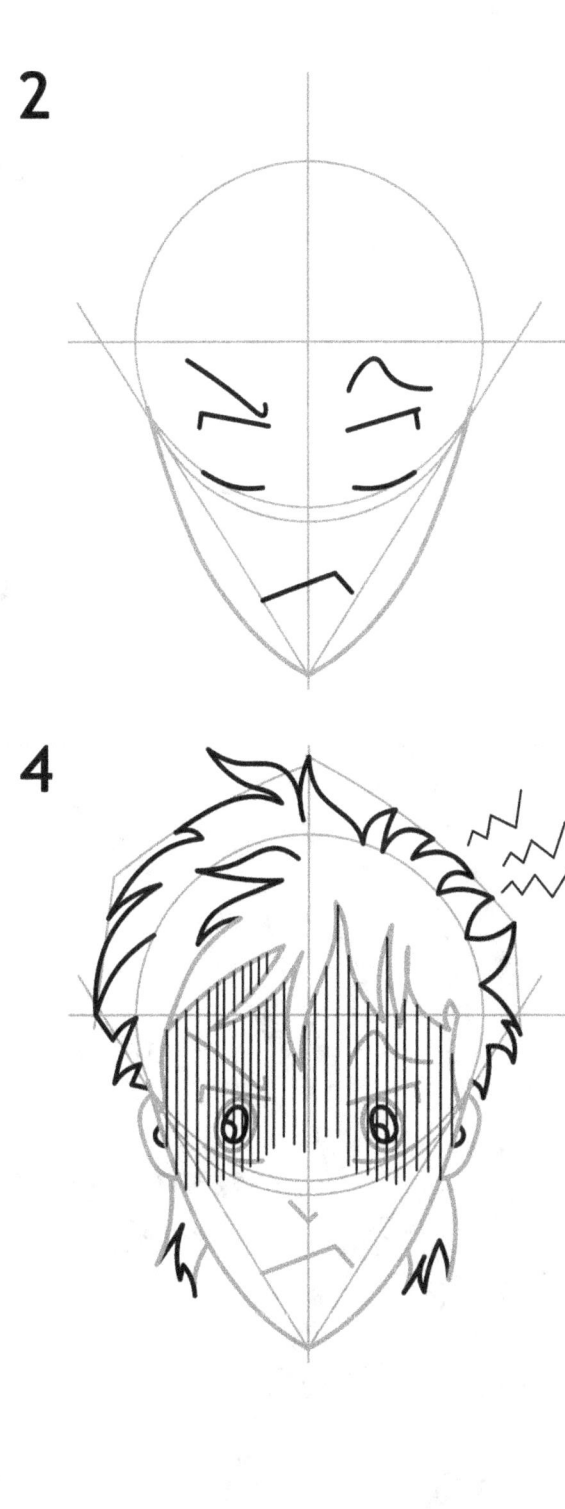

27. Bored Girl

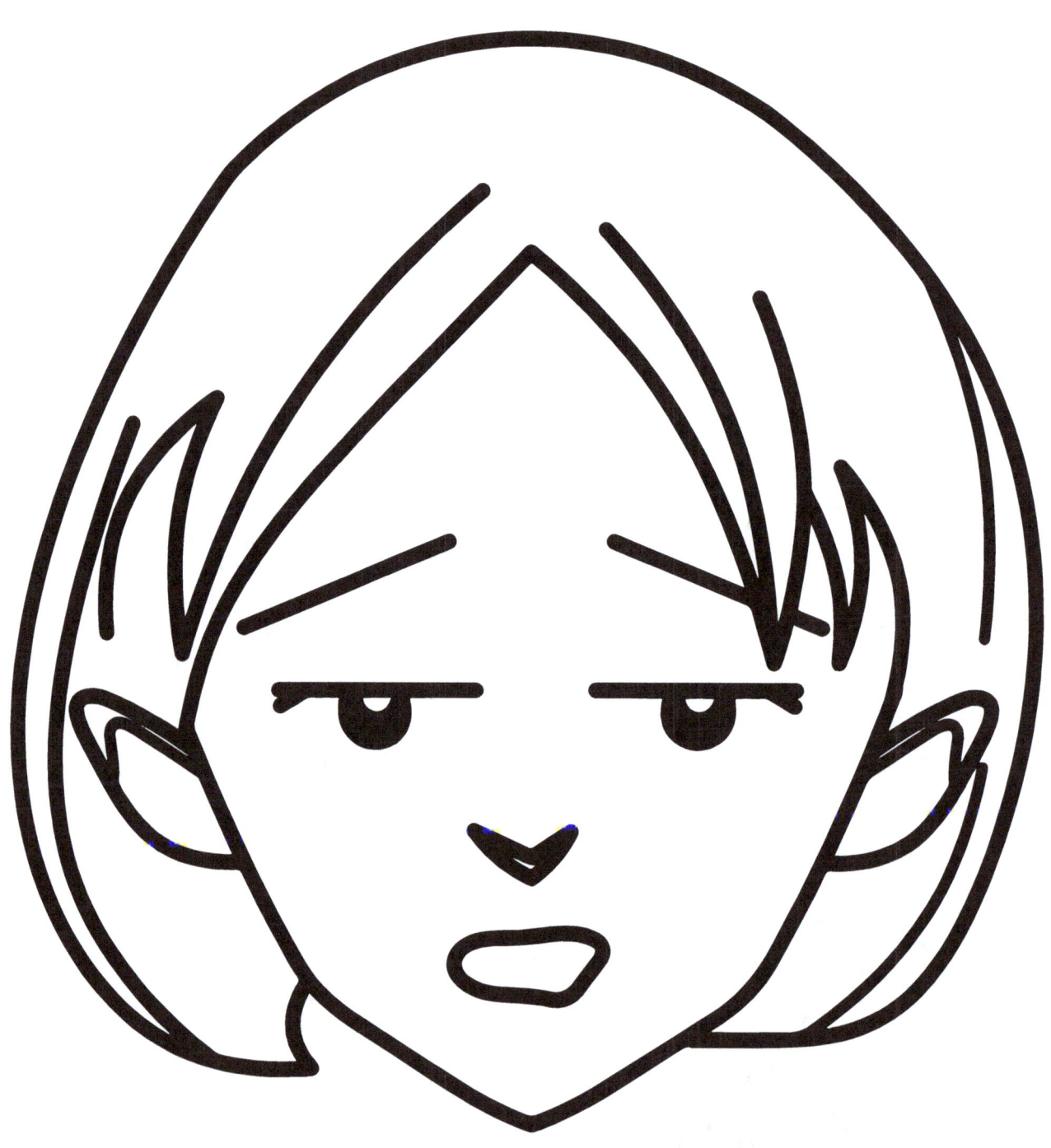

Eyebrows are raised upwards by straight lines. The upper eyelids are also straight lines. The pupils are small. Mouth is in the form of an uneven oval.

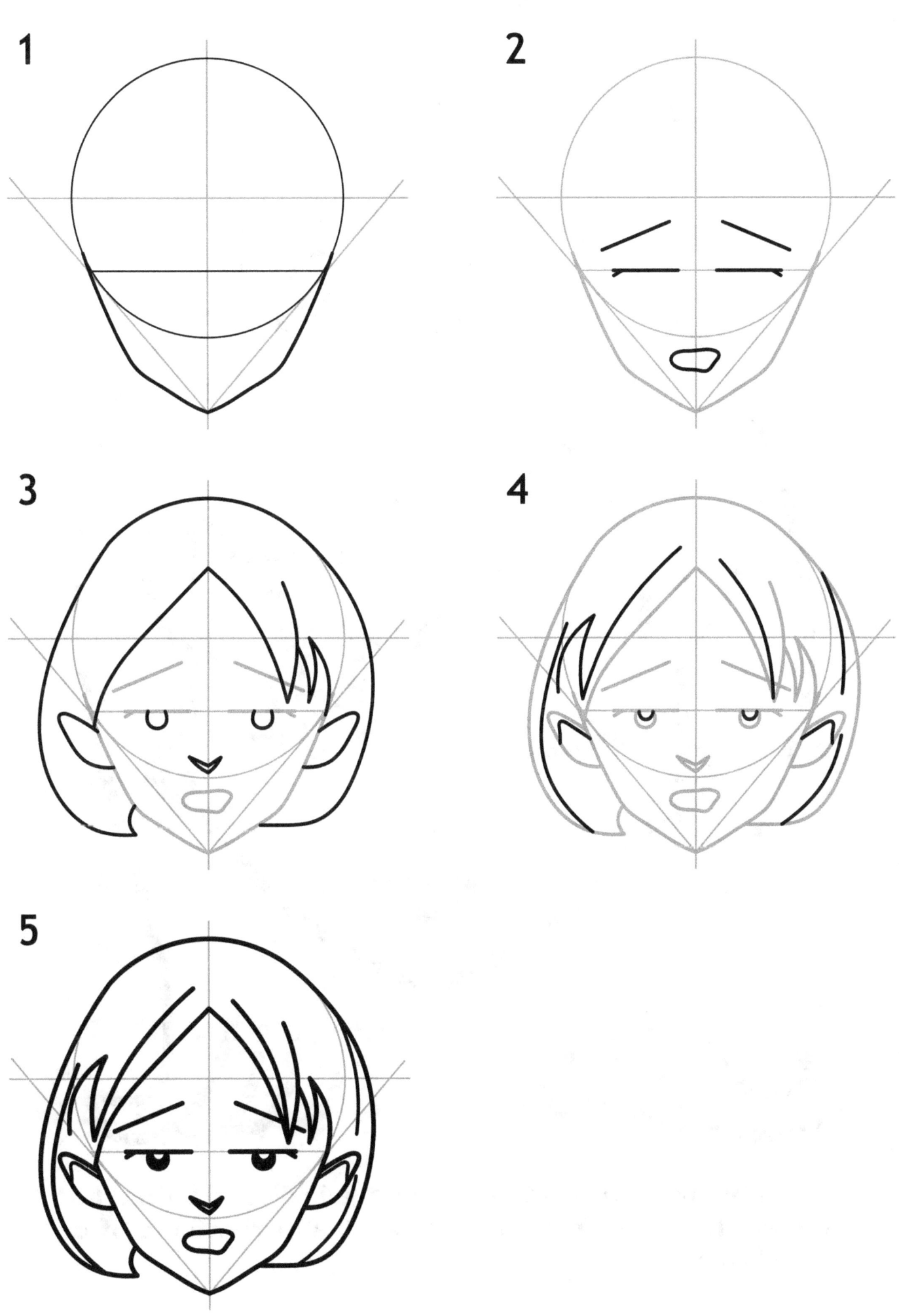

28. Winking Girl

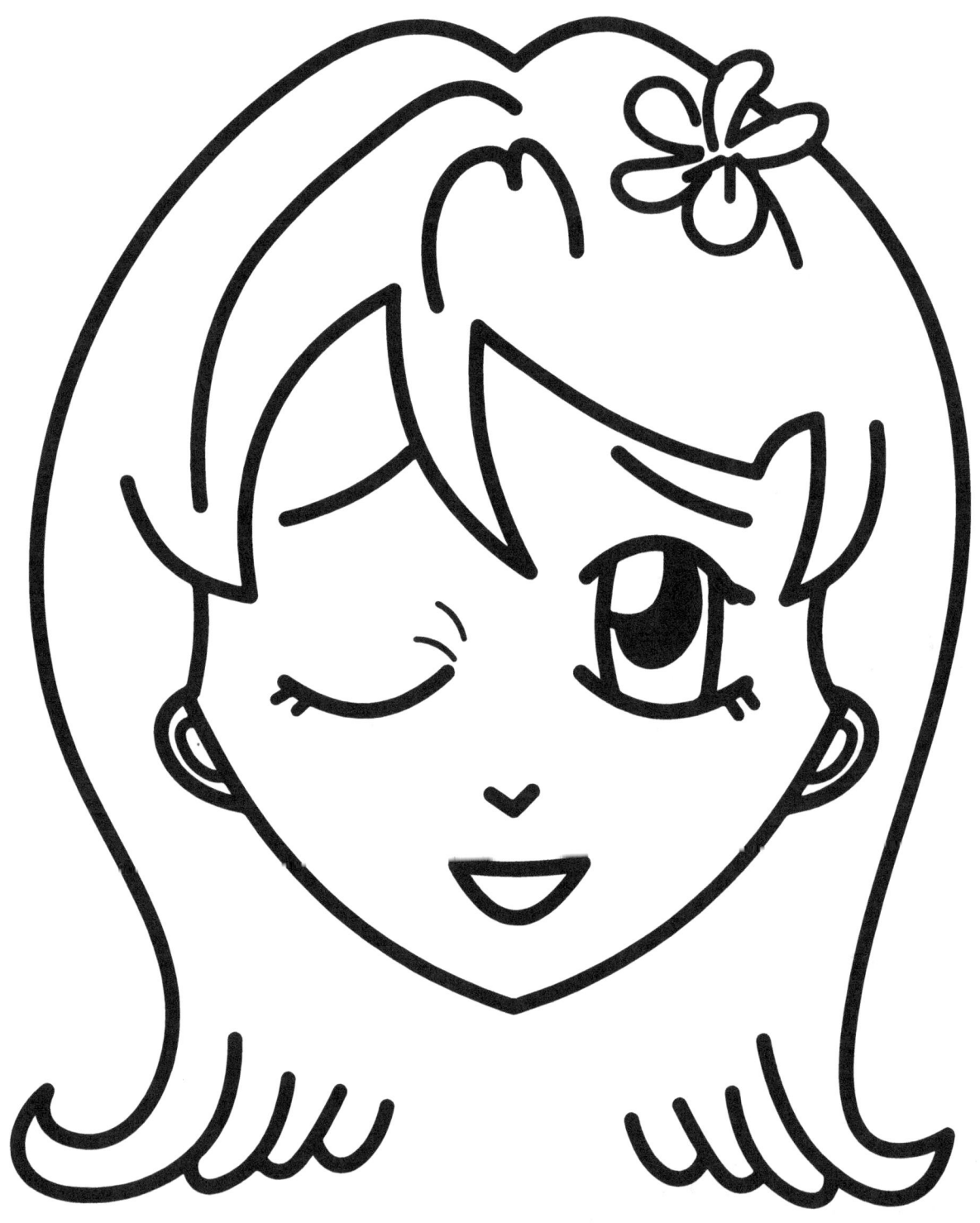

Eyebrows are raised up. One eye is closed with a lid down, the other is opened. Mouth is in the form of a small smile.

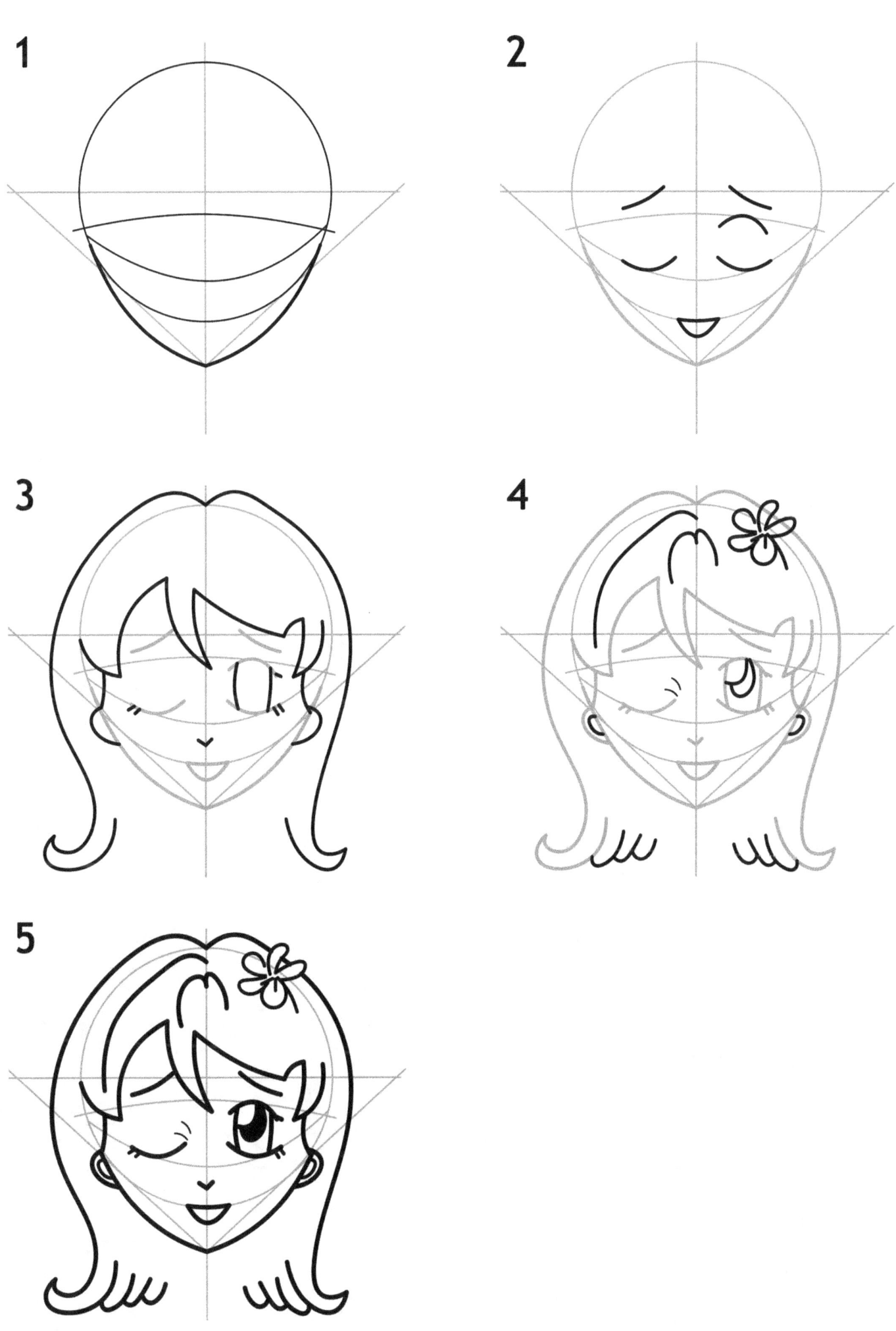

FREE PAGES

THANK YOU for choosing this book, we hope you found it HELPFUL! Feel free to write YOUR REVIEW on AMAZON, we want to know YOUR IMPRESSION!

And we want to GIVE YOU free PAGES from our other books:

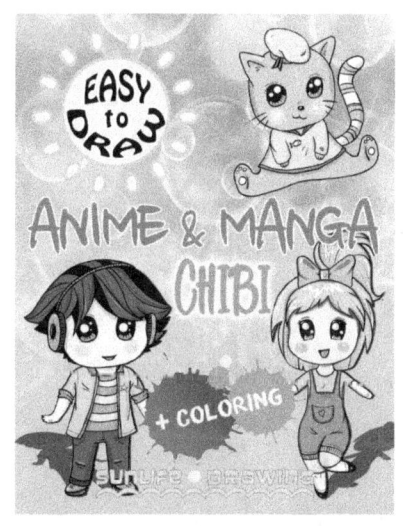

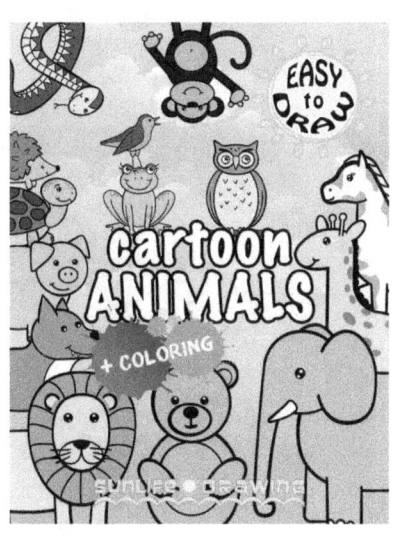

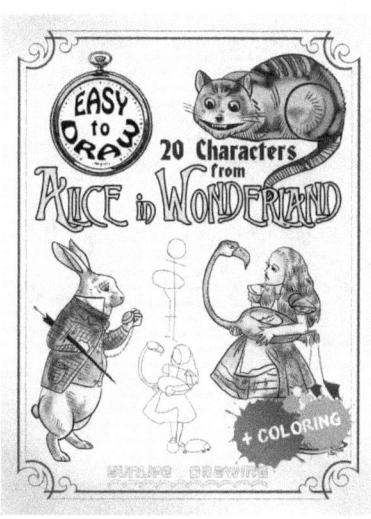

CHIBI JOYFUL GIRL

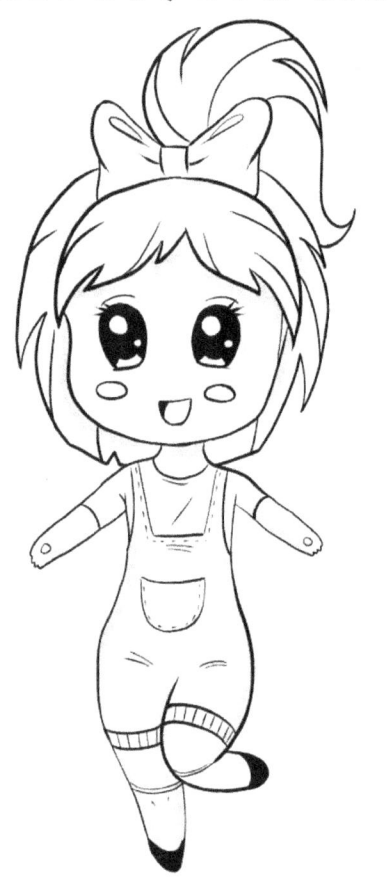

1.

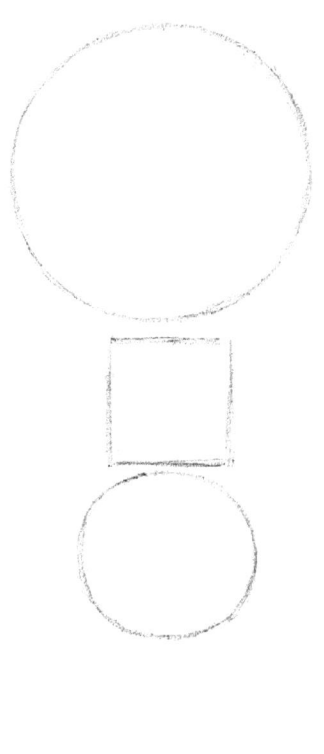

2.

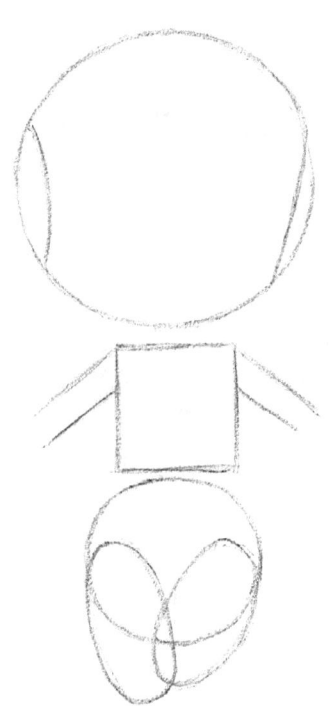

3.

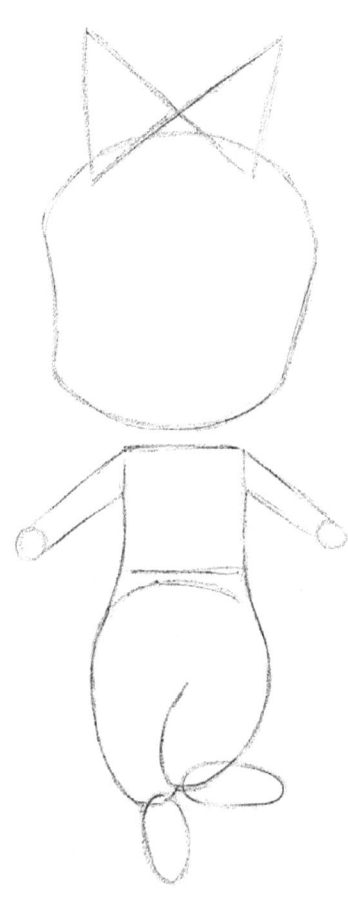

Free Page from the book "EASY to DRAW Anime & Manga CHIBI" © 2017 by Sunlife Drawing

4.

5.

6.

7.

Free Page from the book "EASY to DRAW Anime & Manga CHIBI" © 2017 by Sunlife Drawing

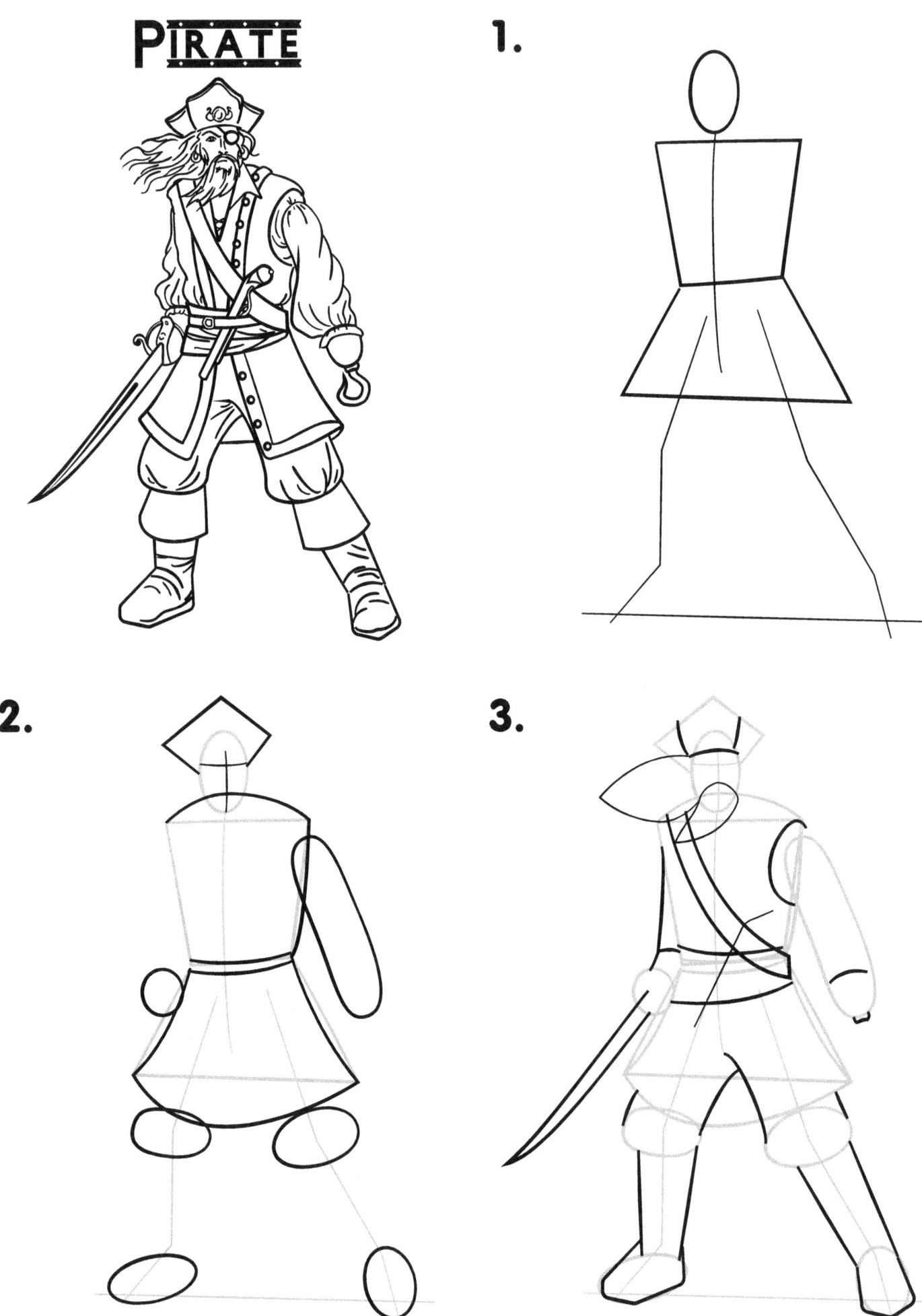

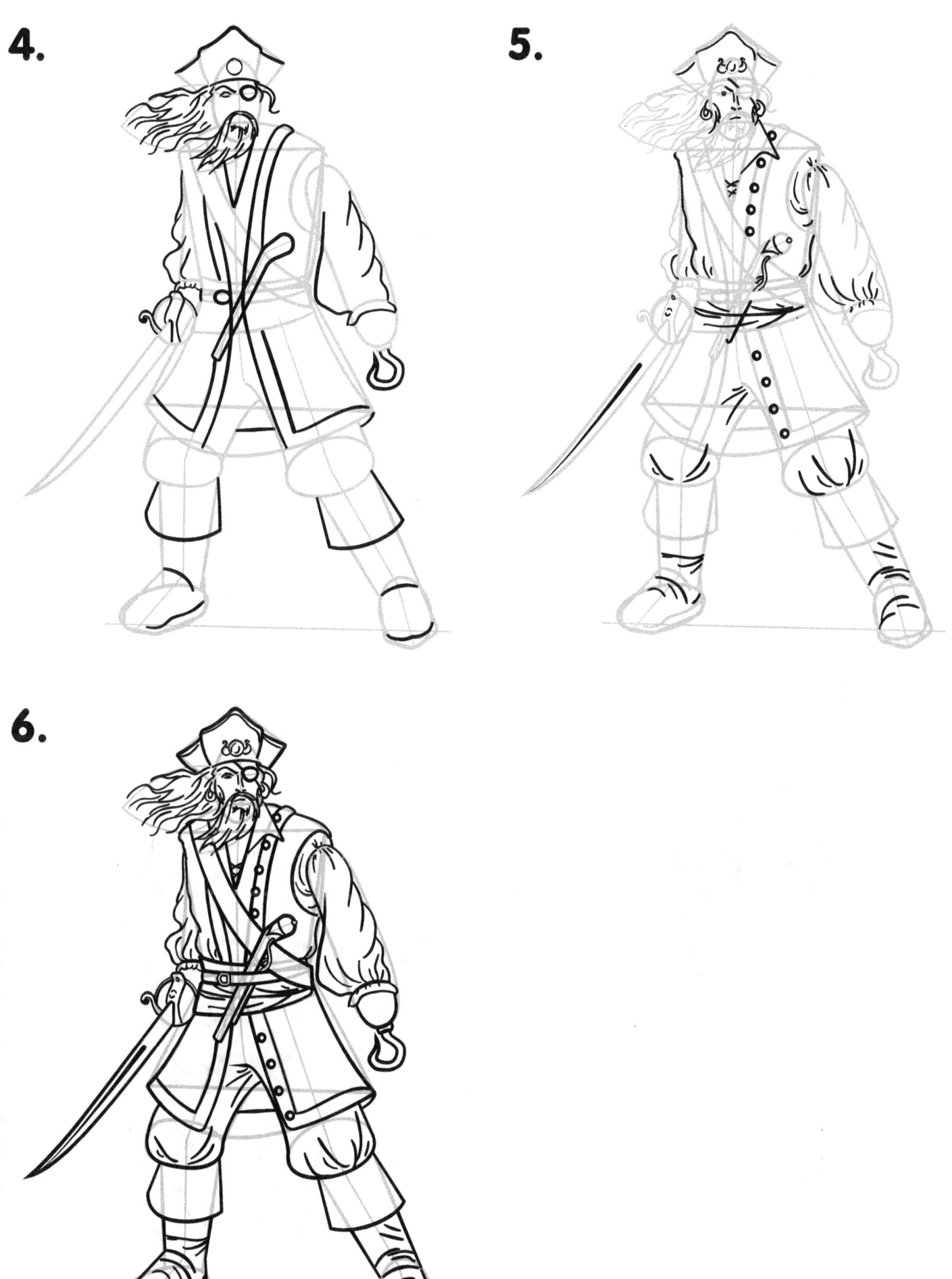

Free Page from the book "The Best BOY's Drawing Book" © 2017 by Sunlife Drawing

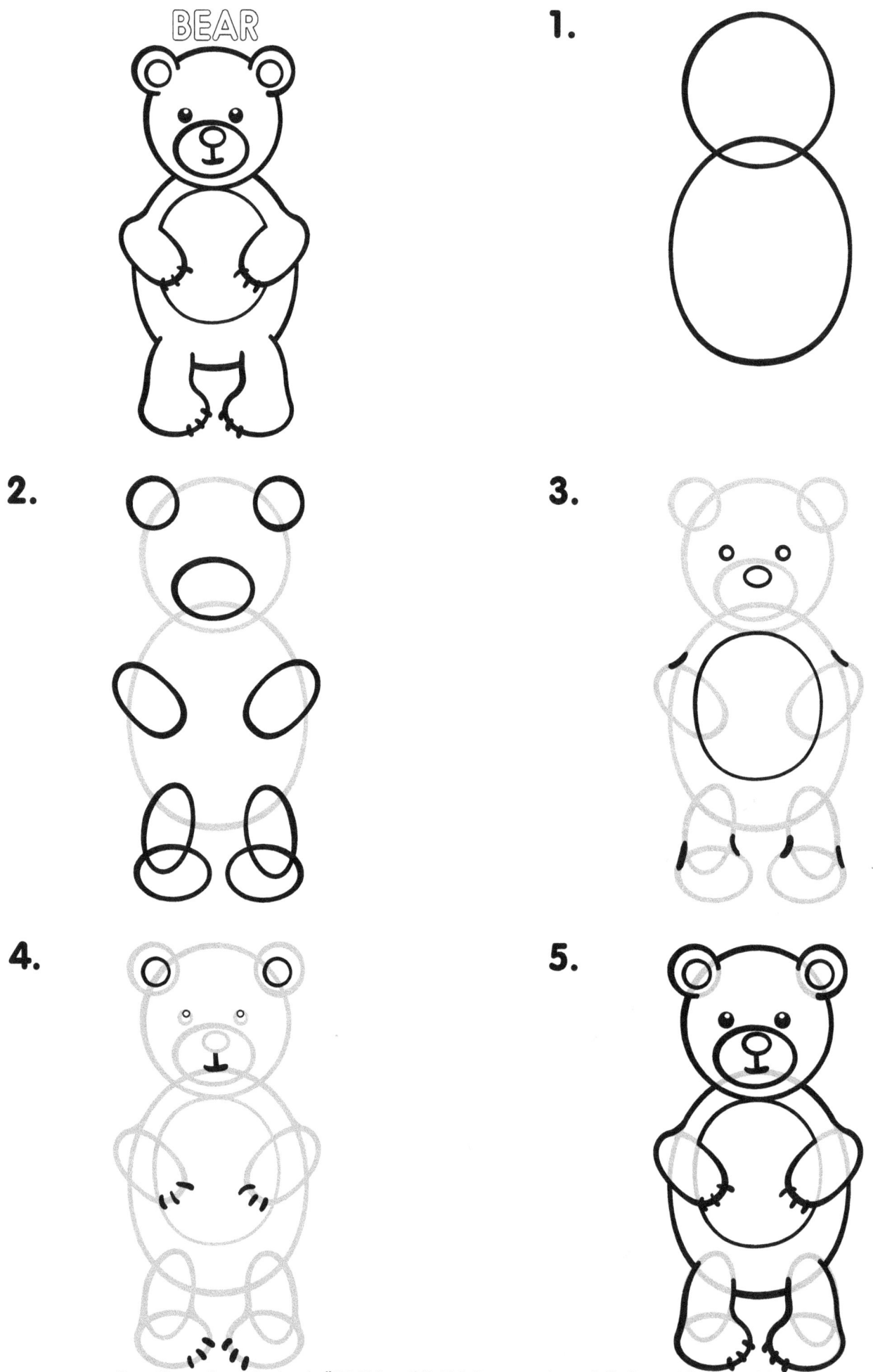

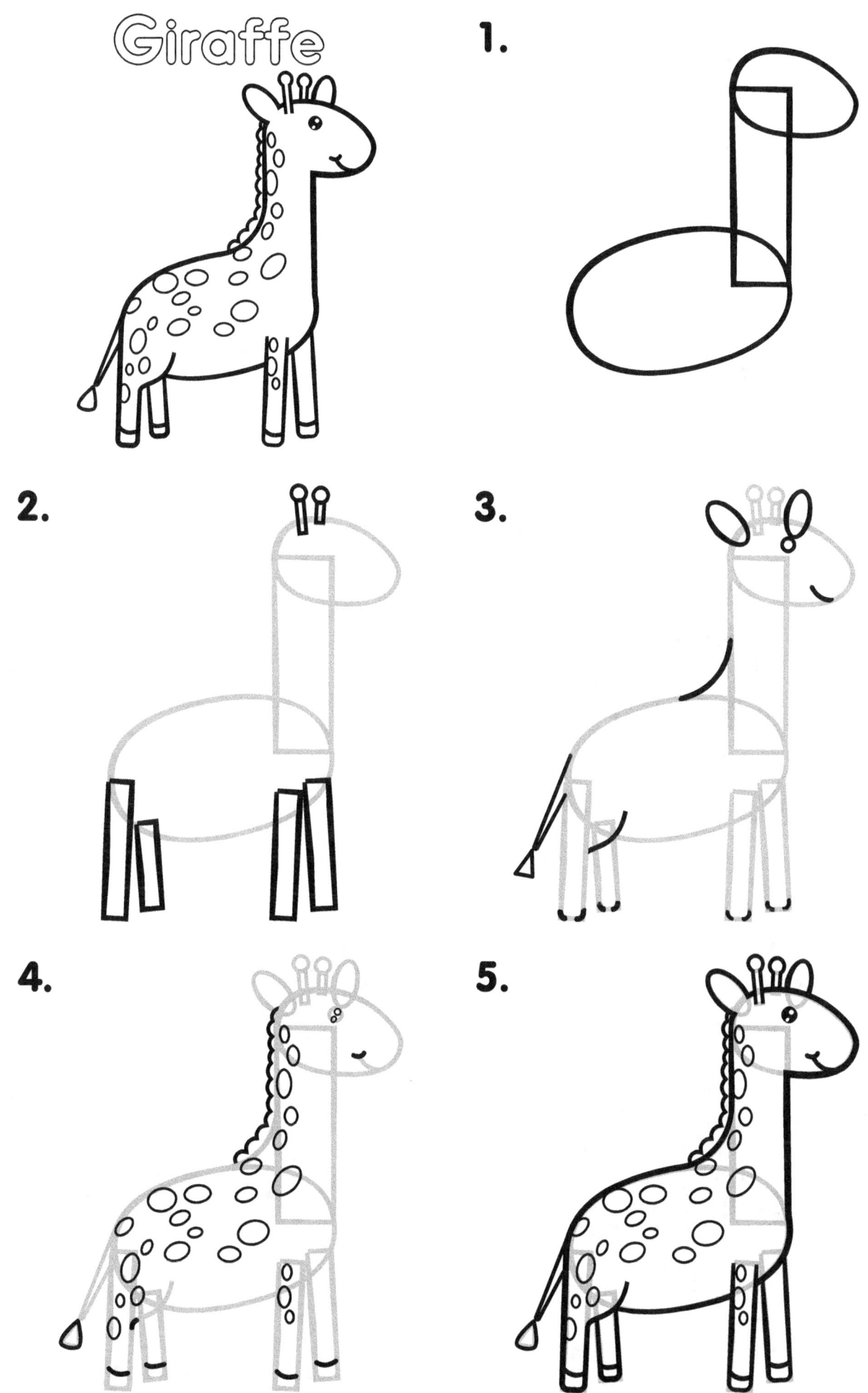

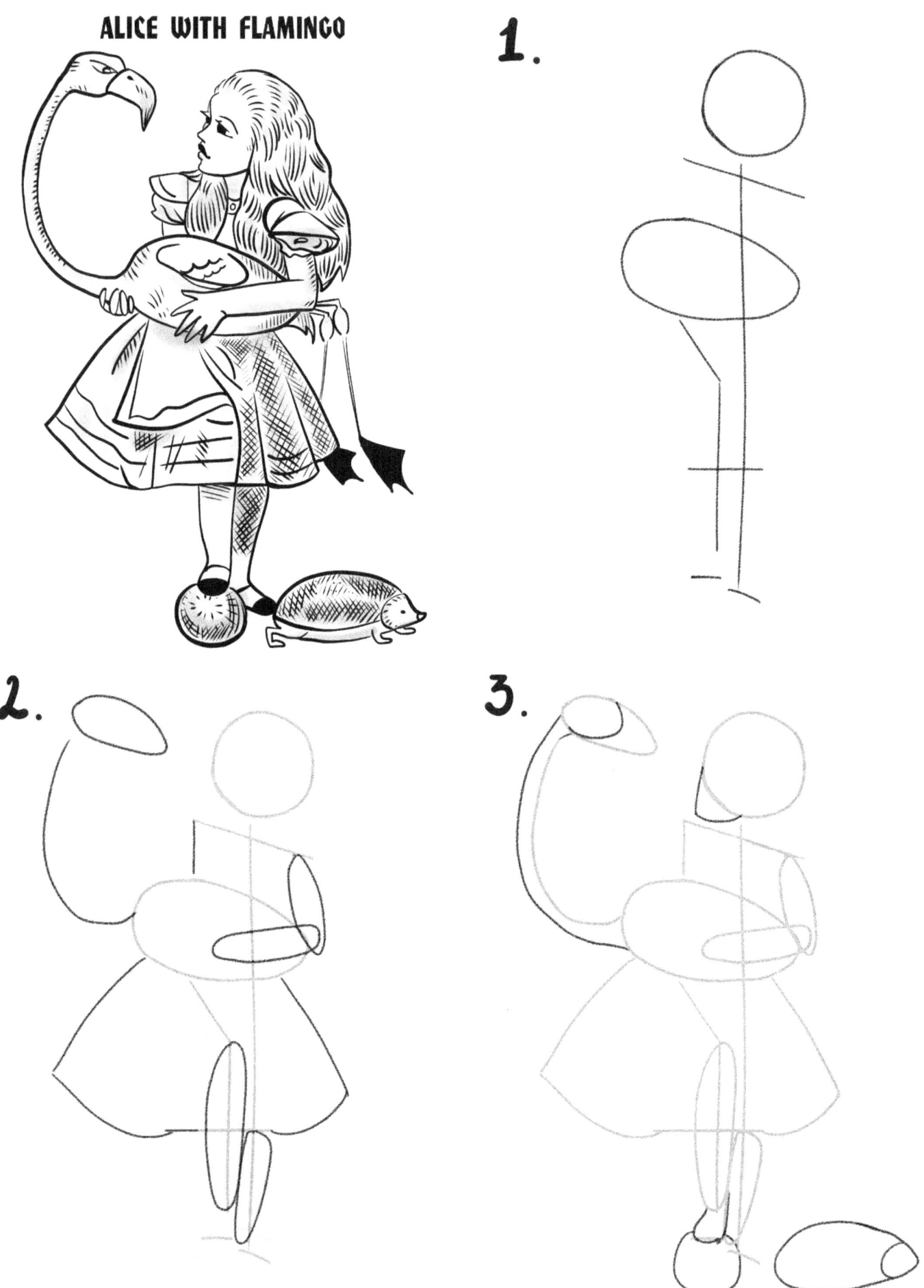

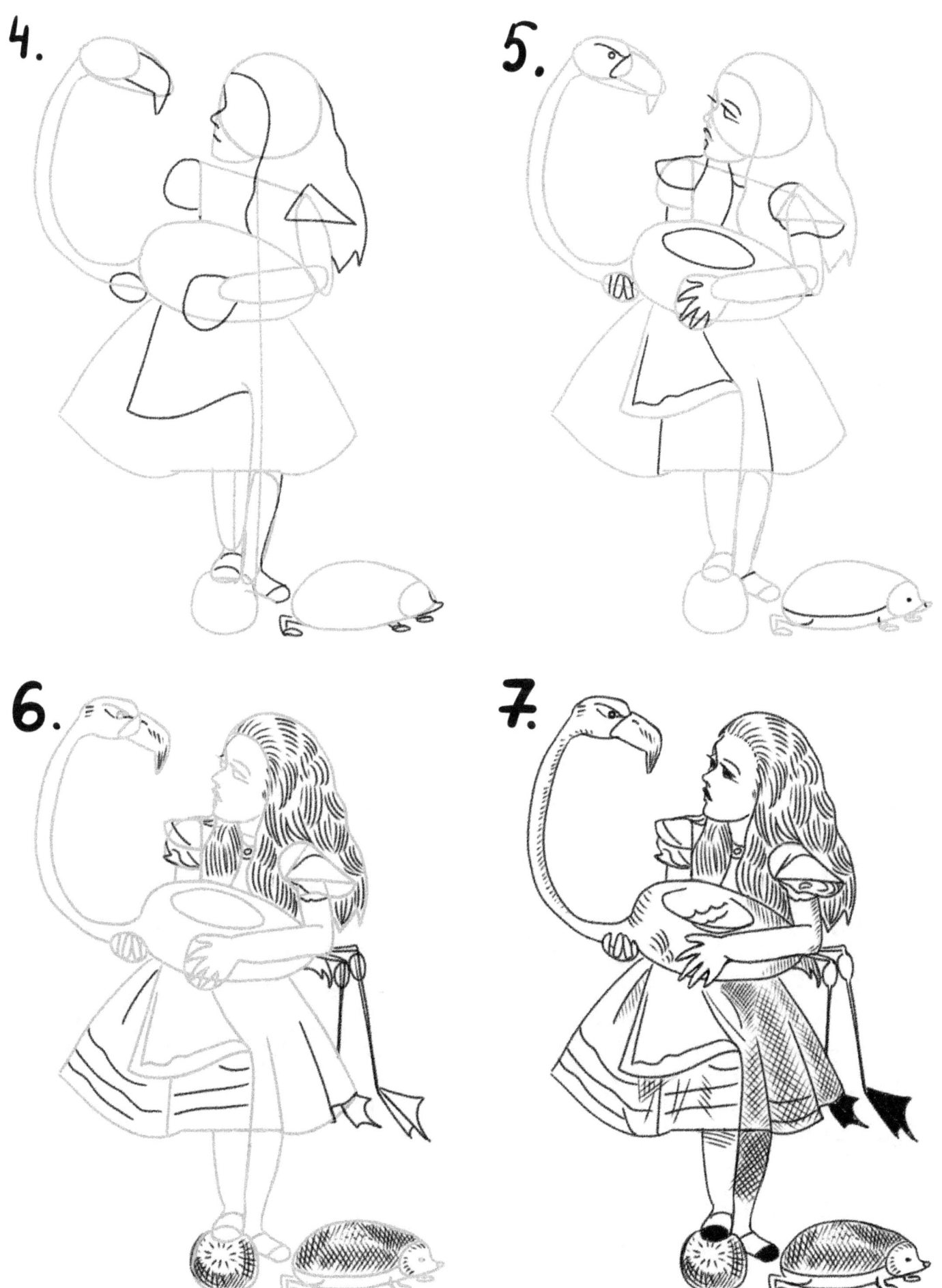

Free Page from the book "EASY to DRAW 20 Characters from Alice in Wonderland" © 2017 by Sunlife Drawing

www.ingramcontent.com/pod-product-compliance
Lightning Source LLC
Chambersburg PA
CBHW080000230526
45470CB00008B/2812